Past-into-Present Series

TRADE UNIONS

Peter Lane

B. T. BATSFORD LTD London

First published 1969
© Peter Lane 1969

Filmset by Keyspools Ltd, Golborne, Lancashire

Printed in Great Britain by Billing & Son Ltd, Guildford, Surrey
for the Publishers
B. T. Batsford Ltd, 4 Fitzhardinge Street, London, W1.

7134 1758 7

Acknowledgments

The author and publisher wish to thank the following for the illustrations appearing in this book: Associated Press Ltd. for fig. 34; Trustees of the British Museum for figs. 2, 18, 19 and 20; Central Office of Information for fig. 72; *The Daily Telegraph* for fig. 1; Ford Motor Co. Ltd. for fig. 57; London Express for figs. 61, 66, 67, 69 and 73; London Museum for fig. 39; Mansell Collection for figs. 5, 9, 11, 12, 13, 14, 15, 21, 27, 28, 30, 32 and 33; National Society of Brushmakers for fig. 7; Newton, Chambers & Co. Ltd. for fig. 3; Popperfoto for fig. 65; Press Association Ltd. for fig. 45; Radio Times Hulton Picture Library for figs. 22, 24, 29, 36, 37, 38, 40, 41, 42, 43, 46, 47, 48, 49, 52, 53, 55, 56, 58, 60, 62, 63 and 64; Sheffield City Libraries for fig. 6; The Times Newspapers for figs. 68, 70, 71 and 75; Topix, Thomson Newspapers for figs. 54 and 75; T.U.C. for figs. 16, 17, 23, 25, 31, 44, 50, 51, 59 and 76.

Contents

Acknowledgment   2
List of Illustrations   3

1. Before the Combination Acts 1799, 1800   5
2. From Peterloo to Tolpuddle   16
3. Model Unions, 1851–1880   28
4. Unions for Unskilled Workers, 1880–1910   35
5. Industrial Unrest, 1910–1914   47
6. From the First World War to the General Strike   54
7. From the General Strike to 1945   66
8. Unions in the Post-War World   74
9. Unions and Modern Economic Planning   80
10. Organisation   90

Index   95

Illustrations

1. Strike headline   5
2. Turnpike road   6
3. Thorncliffe ironworks   7
4. 'Jersey wheel'   9
5. Carding engines and roving machines   9
6. Sheffield, *c*. 1850   10–11
7. Membership certificate   12
8. Gillray's cartoon of Orator Hunt   13
9. Peterloo   14
10. Initiation ceremony   16
11. Francis Place   17
12. Joseph Hume   17
13. Sir Robert Peel   18
14. William Huskisson   18
15. Robert Owen's factory at New Lanark   19
16. Notice issued by Dorchester magistrates   21
17. Meeting at Copenhagen fields   22–23
18. The 'Tolpuddle Martyrs'   24
19. Public dinner to celebrate remission of sentence on 'martyrs'   25
20. Plug riots at Preston   26
21. Opening of Stockton and Darlington railway   28–29
22. Outing at Shirley Hills   29
23. Robert Applegarth, William Allen and George Odger   30

257274

24	Bringing in foreign workers	31
25	First Trade Union Congress	32
26	Beaconsfield Buildings, Islington	33
27	Slum in Glasgow	35
28	Bethnal Green Employment Association	36
29	Matchmakers	36
30	Waiting for work at the docks	37
31	Dockers' Manifesto	38
32	Dockers' march through London	39
33	Violence during railway strike, 1891	40
34	Matchbox maker	41
35	Pawnshop in Merthyr Tydfil, 1873	42
36	Keir Hardie speaking in Trafalgar Square, 1913	43
37	Girls on strike	44
38	Clerks striking	45
39	The right dishonourable double-face Asquith	47
40	Ben Tillett addresses strikers, 1912	49
41	Welsh miners being welcomed by A. J. Cook, 1927	50
42	Women working as window cleaners	51
43	John Hodge	52
44	Harry Gosling	54
45	The Dockers' K.C., Ernest Bevin, 1920	54
46	Going to the pawnshop, 1921	55
47	Winston Churchill on his way to present his Budget, 1925	57
48	Herbert Smith, the miners' leader	58
49	Armoured cars carrying foor during General Strike, 1926	60
50	Nottingham miners decide which union to join	61
51	Citrine	62
52	Transport House	63
53	Sir Alfred Mond	64
54	Ben Turner	65
55	J. M. Keynes	66
56	Working at Morris Motors	67
57	Union-management meeting at Fords	68
58	A.E.U. send supplies to Spanish refugees, 1939	69
59	Ernest Bevin in 1940	70
60	Beveridge in 1942	71
61	Low's carthorse	72
62	Election night, 1945	74
63	Harold Wilson and Stafford Cripps, 1950	75
64	Sir (later Lord) Monckton	76
65	Harold Macmillan	78
66	Conservative freedom versus a planned economy	79
67	Britain and the Common Market	80
68	First Meeting of N.E.D.C., 1962	81
69	Vicky's cartoon of Enoch Powell as Minister of Health	82
70	Signing of Declaration of Intent, 1964	83
71	George Woodcock signing joint agreement on productivity, 1967	84
72	Ray Gunter, Minister of Labour, at opening of Government Training Centre	85
73	Teachers threaten to strike	87
74	Bank clerks picketing bank, 1967	89
75	Trade-union executives at Central Hall	90–91
76	T.U.C. Training College	93

1 Before the Combination Acts 1799, 1800

The front page of today's newspapers is dominated by the news of a threatened strike. On other pages are reports of union discussions with the government's Prices and Incomes Board, negotiations with various employers and preparations for the forthcoming Labour Party Conference. Today is not unusual; almost every day the newspapers have one or more stories about trade union activities. Often we see photographs of mass meetings of union members, of picket lines outside factories, shops or banks, of union leaders in consultations with their members or with employers.

Today trade union leaders and their members are allowed to meet openly, to act in any legal way they think fit to further the interests of their members and to take part in decision-making at factory, local government and national level. It was not always so. There was a time when trade unions did not exist;

1 The main headline from *The Daily Telegraph*, 26 July, 1968. Similar headlines have appeared since then referring to strikes or threats of strikes in the steel industry, by Post Office workers, by teachers and others.

LONDON, FRIDAY, JULY 26, 1968.

COUSINS ORDERS 'FROZEN £1' BUS MEN'S STRIKE

77,000 ready to stop on Aug 12

Mr. Frank Cousins.

and when they came into being they were small, weak societies, which public opinion, employers and governments distrusted and tried to suppress.

The Early Gilds

When did unions begin? As with many questions in the study of history there is no 'one date' answer. In medieval times most industry was controlled by craft gilds. A young boy would become an apprentice to a master craftsman, who would teach him the 'mysteries' of the craft. When the gild leaders were satisfied that the apprentice had learned his lessons well, he was allowed to become a journeyman, paid a wage by a master craftsman. In time he would bring some of his work to the gild leaders, and if they were satisfied that this was worthy to be called a 'master's piece' they would allow him to set up as a master craftsman, taking on young apprentices.

In the woollen and other craft industries every man could become a master craftsman and employer in time, provided he had the ability, and saved the little money required for the simple tools of his trade.

From the thirteenth century onwards, however, more capital was required to set up in business as industry became more complex; the existing masters made it more difficult for their journeymen to enter their ranks (e.g. by charging very high admission fees). So journeymen remained wage-earning employees.

In several large industrial centres, such as London and Norwich, journeymen

2 This is an eighteenth-century drawing of the Brighton–Henfield road, built and maintained by a turnpike trust. The wide grass verge was used to make detours when the rough road was deeply rutted by rain from the surrounding hills.

3 The Thorncliffe ironworks painted in 1811. In the centre is the blast furnace where Abraham Darby's coke-smelting process was used; the steam engine-house is behind the furnace. Notice the rural surroundings of an early nineteenth-century Sheffield industry.

in the same craft often combined to form a journeyman's gild. This was, in part, a type of friendly society; members paid their subscriptions and were entitled to receive benefits from their gild when sick or unemployed, while the gild would pay for the deceased member's funeral. Some local gilds linked with similar gilds in other towns to form a national network. One of these, the Woolcombers, used to let its members know where work could be had, and would pay the expenses of an unemployed member travelling to seek work.

One obstacle to the formation of such national gild-unions was the difficulty of communications. The primitive road conditions made travel a hard, costly and slow process. During the early eighteenth century it took almost a week to travel from London to York. News of work available in York would arrive in London and be sent out to members who might then travel to York. The whole process would take about three or four weeks and by this time perhaps the vacancies had been filled.

The journeyman gilds soon came into conflict with the master craftsmen, their employers. During the seventeenth century there were a large number of organised strikes as the workers tried to obtain higher wages during a period of rising prices. When the gilds concerned themselves with hours and conditions of work, wages and piece-rates, they were, in fact, behaving like a trade union.

Workmen's Associations

Some industries never had the apprentice-to-journeyman-to-master system of gild control. In the coal industry, for example, someone had to spend a large sum of money developing a mine before any coal could be dug out. The blast furnace had to be built and paid for before any iron could be produced. In such capitalist industries few workmen could hope to become masters and owners. A working class grew up in areas where such industries were found, and these workers often combined to form local workmen's associations. A member of such an association would pay his entry fee and a weekly subscription, and receive some of the friendly society benefits which gilds gave their members. His membership of the association would be attested by a card.

These associations often came into conflict with the employers. In 1662 the pitmen from the mines in the district around the Tyne and the Wear sent a petition to Parliament asking for some improvement to be made in the regulations concerning their system of 'hiring'. In 1765 the miners from Northumberland and Durham came out on strike against the owners' abuse of the system, by which an owner was supposed to hire a workman for a year for an agreed wage. Many owners tried to lengthen the period of hiring which might mean that a man's wage would not rise even though the cost of goods had.

Local Trade Unions

The industrial changes of the second half of the eighteenth century led to the decline of the domestic system of industry and the growth of large factories. In the domestic system, spinning wheels were to be found in many cottages. These workers were less conscious of their common plight than the larger number of workers in the factories. Workers in one factory would also have similar interests to workers in other factories in the towns which grew up in industrial England. In Sheffield, as **6** shows, there were many factories, so that there would be many workmen in close contact with each other and having the same grievances against their employers.

This led to the formation of many local trade unions. Sheffield grinders, Bolton weavers, Dorchester agricultural labourers, the names of many early unions show that their members came only from a particular locality, largely owing to the problem of communications. They were also craft unions, their

4 This big wheel or 'Jersey wheel' was found in most cottages in pre-industrialised England. The old lady on the left is busy winding yarn into skeins for weaving. There was little need for skill or training in this simple industrial scene.

5 Carding engines *(left)* and drawing and roving machines *(right)* in this engraving of 1843 prepare the cotton for spinning. The size and cost of the machines account for the growth of factories.

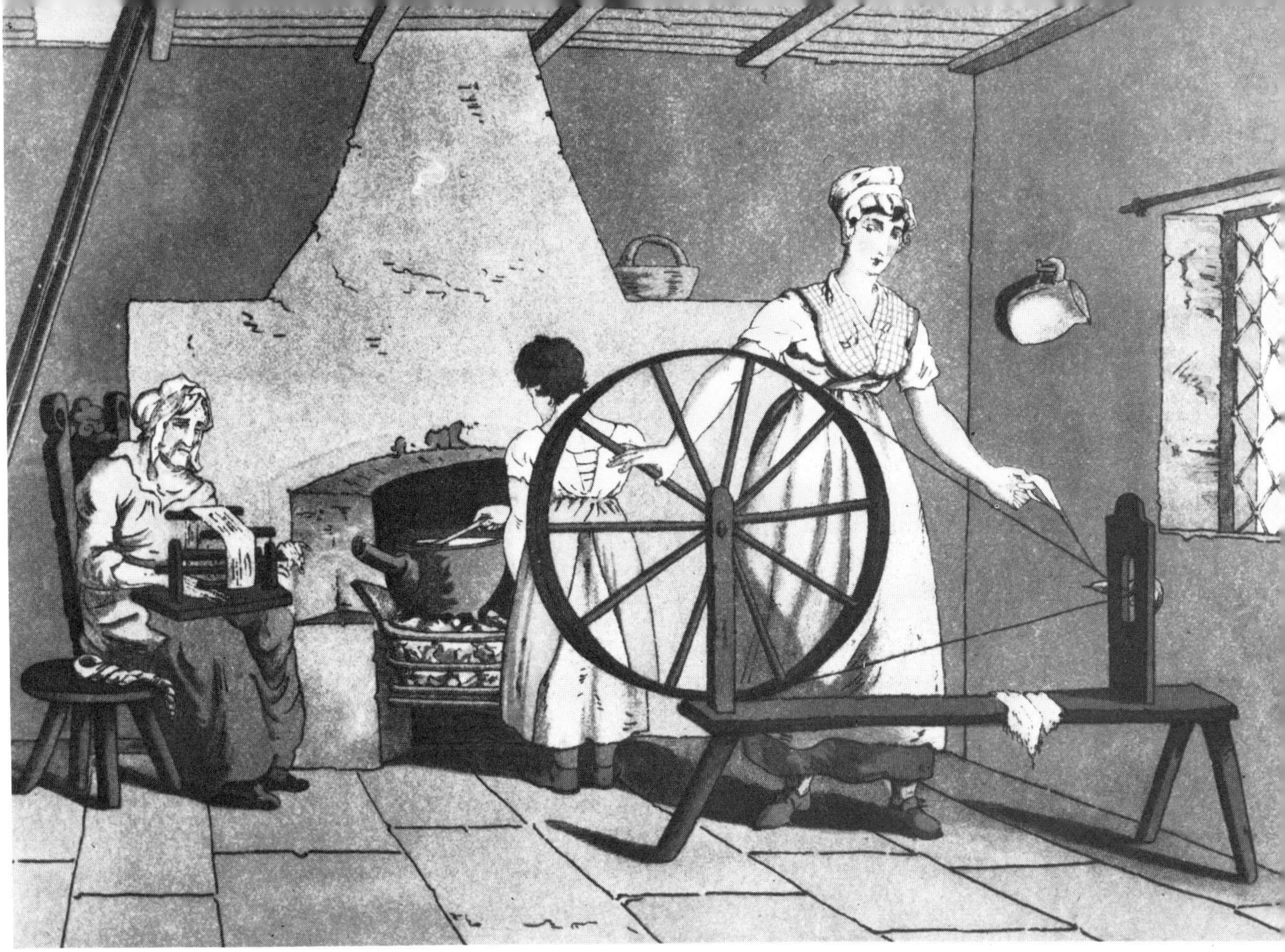

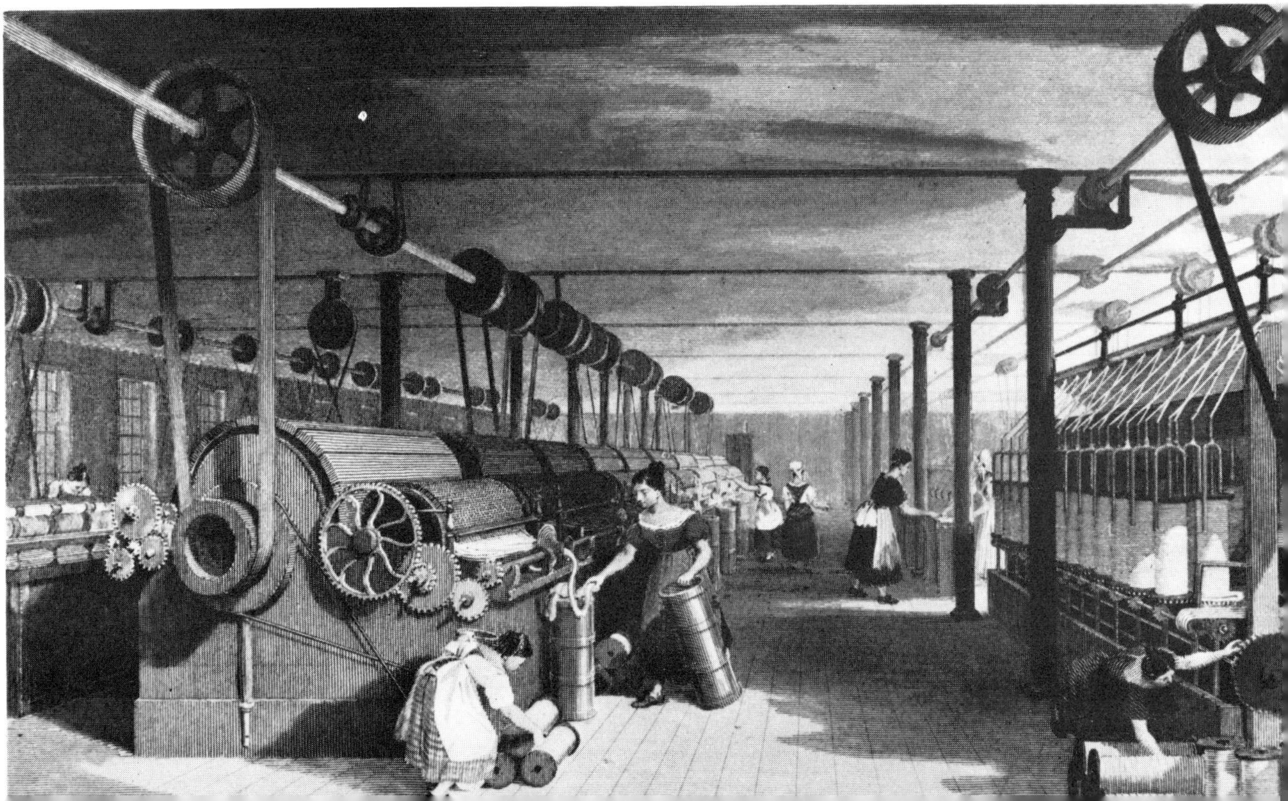

6 Sheffield was one of the towns that grew rapidly in the nineteenth century. This painting (*c.* 1850)

gives an impression of smoke and lack of planning.

members being people doing the same work, having served the same apprenticeship and having common interests. They were anxious to maintain, or increase, the level of wages which might lead to an improvement in their social conditions and enable them to afford better housing, more food, better clothing. The unions also tried to improve industrial conditions, to get employers to agree to shorter working hours, or, as in the case of the miners, to better hiring agreements; they campaigned against the system of fining late-comers by which some employers reduced workers' wages. Two of the main targets for many unions were the tommy or company shop where they were forced to buy goods, often at high prices, and the system of paying wages in kind, known as the truck system.

Many of these unions carried on several of the practices of the journeyman

7 A certificate of membership issued by the brushmakers' union in September 1830 to a Leicester workman who had completed his apprenticeship.

8 Gillray mocks Orator Hunt and similar reformers; the mob surrounding them are drawn to resemble pigs or empty-headed oafs. In the left-hand corner little slave boys sign a petition already signed by Wat Tyler.

gilds. They paid benefits to less fortunate members, they insisted that new entrants into their craft should have served an adequate apprenticeship, while they also tried to limit the number entering an apprenticeship. In so doing they tried to make sure that existing craftsmen would have enough work at good wages.

Radicalism and Repression

While these unions were being formed and were campaigning in the late eighteenth and early nineteenth centuries, other movements were also active. The Luddites tried to prevent the introduction of machinery into the textile industries; the Radicals were campaigning for law reform, for a press free from tax and censorship, and, above all, for Parliamentary Reform. Many workers went to meetings of all three movements, so that a union member might be a machine-breaking Luddite one day, and attend a Radical demonstration the next. The 'respectable' public certainly linked all three movements together,

9 This memorial was presented to Henry Hunt to commemorate the 'wanton and furious attack made by that brutal armed force the Manchester and Cheshire Yeomanry Cavalry' at St Peter's Field, Manchester, on 16 August, 1819. This portrayal of the radicals contrasts strongly with Gillray's.

and imagined that this Radical movement was dangerous.

This belief helps to explain Parliament's attitude towards the union movement at the end of the eighteenth century. In 1721 the Master Tailors of London had petitioned Parliament for an Act to stop combination (or union) among their journeymen. Parliament, having heard both sides in the dispute, ruled that such combination was unlawful, fixed the hours of work at 13, fixed maximum wages at 2s. per day in April, May and June and 1s. 8d. for the rest of the year, and said that the Justices of the Peace could alter the wage rates at future meetings of Quarter Sessions.

Notice that Parliament and the Justices claimed the power to fix wage rates. This claim, inherited from the Tudor period (if not earlier), could be made good in the smaller, more stable society of pre-industrial England. Even then it had led to strikes in the seventeenth century. But in the industrial society of the late eighteenth century, with very much larger factories and greater numbers of workers in more varied occupations, Parliament and the Justices could not regulate comprehensively as they had once done.

However, Parliament and the Justices were not willing to give up their claims easily. And a Parliament which had seen the revolt of the American colonies in the 1770s, an upsurge of popular support for radical Wilkes in the 1780s, the French Revolution in the early 1790s and a naval mutiny and Irish revolt in the late 1790s, was easily frightened. The Gillray cartoon (**8**) gives an idea of 'respectable' people's opinions of popular movements.

It was a respectable, frightened Parliament which in April 1799 heard a petition from the London master millwrights against a combination of London journeymen millwrights. This was in some ways a repetition of the petition of 1721—a local union, a local group of employers and an appeal to Parliament. On 8 April, 1799 Sir John Anderson, MP moved 'that leave be given to bring in a Bill to prevent unlawful combination of workmen employed in the millwright business, and to enable the magistrates to regulate their wages within certain limits'. The remedy proposed was, again, very similar to that proposed in 1721.

During the debate on this motion, William Wilberforce, the leader of the campaign against slavery and the slave trade asked 'whether it might not be advisable to extend the principles of this motion, and to make it general against combination of all workers'. This combination he regarded as a general disease in our society.

By 17 June, 1799 Pitt, the Prime Minister, had accepted Wilberforce's advice and agreed to 'bring in a Bill to prevent unlawful combination of workmen'. And so the Combination Acts of 1799 and 1800 came into being. The first forbade the formation of unions if these aimed at improving wage rates, altering hours of work or conditions of employment. The second specifically forbade strikes, union meetings or the collection of union subscriptions.

In this way did Parliament and the 'respectable' section of the population hope to deal with this growing threat. Parliament passed such laws, Justices and judges dealt out severe sentences to those found guilty of breaking them. It was in this atmosphere of fear and repression that the union movement continued to grow, that Radical demonstrations continued to be held and that incidents such as that at St. Peter's Field (or Peterloo) took place.

Further Reading
J. L. and B. Hammond: *The Town Labourer, 1760–1832* (Longmans)
G. D. Cole and R. W. Postgate: *The Common People, 1746–1946* (Methuen)
T. S. Ashton: *The Industrial Revolution, 1760–1830* (H.U.L.)

2 From Peterloo to Tolpuddle

Describing conditions after the passing of the Combination Acts, Francis Place said that:

> could an accurate account be given of hearings before magistrates, trials at Sessions and in the Court of King's Bench, the gross injustices and the terrible punishments would not be credited.

Thousands of arrests were made and heavy sentences passed during the frenzy of the Napoleonic Wars and the panic of the years 1815–22. But many unions remained in being. The London Millwrights, for example, held meetings throughout this time. As industry continued to grow, industrial towns expanded and ever larger numbers of workers lived and worked together, sharing the same economic and social miseries, lacking legal and political rights. It was almost inevitable that they should unite.

Many unions disguised themselves as Friendly and Benevolent Clubs or Societies; Friendly Societies were formed by the Ironmongers in 1809, the Turners in 1812 and the Bradford Mechanics in 1822. Old unions and new societies had to conduct their affairs in secret. A pamphlet written in 1834, *The Character, Object and Effects of Trades Unions*, gives a vivid account of a union meeting. There were, of course, no photographers present, but the artist's impression (**10**) is a faithful representation of what actually took place. When

10 An artist's impression of an initiation into a trade union in the early nineteenth century.

11 *(left)* Francis Place (1771–1854). Place campaigned for trade-union reform, the Reform Act (1832) and educational reform. **12** *(right)* Joseph Hume MP was an invaluable ally for Place.

the Huddersfield Mechanics formed a new branch in 1831 their first purchase was curtains, to prevent people peeping into their clubroom, a Bible, on which members took an oath of loyalty and secrecy, and a pistol to ensure that this oath was kept. They would not have thought that the artist was exaggerating.

Repeal of the Combination Acts

Francis Place had been a journeyman in the breech-making trade; in 1793 he had led a strike of fellow journeymen. Having spent five years as a trade union organiser, he set up as a self-employed tailor in Charing Cross (1799), but continued to support the workers' claims. His shop became well known as a meeting place for Radicals, free-thinking politicians, philosophers and writers. With their assistance Place began a campaign to change public opinion concerning unions, and, in particular, to change the opinions held by MPs and members of the Tory government. One of his main supporters in this work was Joseph Hume MP. He and Place were fortunate when, in 1822, Canning, Peel and

13 *(left)* Sir Robert Peel had a more flexible attitude to reform and helped to create a more favourable attitude to Place's agitations. **14** *(right)* William Huskisson, President of the Board of Trade 1822–28, was responsible for the repeal of the Combination Acts.

Huskisson replaced Castlereagh, Eldon and Sidmouth in Lord Liverpool's government. The government was still led by Liverpool, it was still a Tory government, but the newcomers soon showed that the policy of the Cabinet had changed. Huskisson relaxed the application of the Navigation Acts, began the movement towards Free Trade by lowering tariffs, and even talked of altering the Corn Laws; Peel reformed the Criminal Code and the conditions in prisons, and abolished the death penalty for many crimes. It was a government of reformers, and Place and Hume hoped that it might look favourably on their proposal to allow Hume to introduce a private member's Bill repealing the Combination Acts.

Huskisson was not willing to go this far; in 1824 he did, however, appoint Hume to lead a Select Committee into 'the Emigration of Artisans, the Exportation of Machinery,' and (tacked on to the end) 'the law on Workmen's Combination'. At the end of 1824 an Act 'to repeal the laws relating to combination of workmen' went through Parliament, almost unnoticed by most MPs.

The period 1822–27 was one of industrial expansion; foreign trade grew rapidly as Britain began to become the 'Workshop of the World'. It was this prosperity which, in part, helped the Liberal Tories to have their way—in the booming years the fear of revolution died out; affluence bred tolerance.

Unemployment fell, wages rose. Working people mistakenly thought that this had something to do with the recognition by Parliament of trade unions. New unions were formed, old ones came out into the open; strikes became more frequent and violent. The employers and 'respectable' opinion were again frightened at the prospect of mob violence. In March 1825 Huskisson ordered a new Committee of Inquiry into the effect of the repeal of the Combination Acts.

Largely owing to the work of Place and Hume, the new Act (1825) allowed men to form unions, but made the unions and their members liable to prosecution under the Common Law; this made it easy for union members to be punished. However, the clock had not gone right back; at least unions could be formed, even though without the freedom which many wanted.

The struggle for recognition was not the whole of the union story in the first years of the nineteenth century. In 1818 the Lancashire spinners had founded the Manchester Philanthropic Society, as a central body to organise the activities of all trades in England. This was a very ambitious scheme in a time of poor communications. The founding of a similar society in London in 1819 shows that not all workers supported the Lancashire scheme, but that many workers wanted some such Grand Union. One of the leaders in this movement towards a Grand National Union was John Doherty, secretary of the Operative Spinners of Lancashire—itself a union much bigger than a mere local union. In 1829 he formed a Grand General Union of Operative Spinners in the United Kingdom— uniting the activities of the spinners of Lancashire, Ireland and Scotland. In 1830 he organised the National Association for the Protection of Labour, supported by unions in 20 different trades, with a membership of 100,000. Doherty's next ambition was to extend this into a truly Grand National Consolidated Union, extending over the whole kingdom and including the members of all trades and unions.

Robert Owen and the G.N.C.T.U.

Robert Owen, like Francis Place, was a self-made man who had risen from the ranks of the working class to become an employer. He had become convinced that the existing capitalist system was wrong, that it set employers against

15 New Lanark in Robert Owen's time showing his model factory and workers' houses. You might compare this picture with **6**.

employees, was the reason for the terrible social and working conditions of the industrial towns. He wrote and spoke of a New Moral Order in which all property would be owned cooperatively, so that private property would be abolished and there would be no employers; he believed that under such a social system everyone would be better treated, happier and lead more moral lives.

It was Robert Owen who took over the leadership of the movement towards a Grand National Union. In February 1834 he set up the Grand National Consolidated Trade Union (G.N.C.T.U.), managed from London by four paid officials. He claimed that he had over 250,000 members from many different trades. Here, it seemed, was a workers' army, which could dictate to the employers and government: from the employers it would obtain higher wages, better conditions of work and improved social conditions; from the government it would get laws to improve the lives of women and children, the quantity and quality of education, treatment of the sick and of the old.

These were some of the claims that Owen made for his Union. He intended to realise these claims by means of the General Strike. It is not surprising that the government and the public were frightened. Some employers drew up 'the document', which spoke of the harm of trade unionism to the employer and the worker and demanded that employees should agree not to join the Union, nor support any striking members by subscriptions or gifts. Every employee had to sign 'the document' when it was presented to him by his employer; refusal to do so led to dismissal.

Other employers were more direct. They simply locked their places of work until the workers had agreed not to join the Union. The worst lock-out was at Derby, in 1833, when 1,500 workers were put out of work. It is obvious that the poorly paid workers were unable to stay out on strike for very long; certainly they were in a less powerful position than the wealthier employers.

Some employers used their influence to get the magistrates to issue notices such as that which appeared at Tolpuddle.

The Tolpuddle Martyrs

In 1833, the magistrates at Tolpuddle met to fix wage rates for the coming year. This was a right which magistrates had always had, but which could no longer be exercised in the growing industrial towns where the number of workers was too great and the variety of work done by different crafts made wage fixing too complicated. In the agricultural areas, however, magistrates still retained this old power.

The farmers at Tolpuddle asked the magistrates to lower the wages from 8s.

16 The Dorchester magistrates issued this warning on 21 February, 1834. The notice ignored the repeal of the Combination Acts and referred to 'illegal societies or unions'. On 24 February the six 'martyrs' were arrested.

CAUTION.

WHEREAS it has been represented to us from several quarters, that mischievous and designing Persons have been for some time past, endeavouring to induce, and have induced, many Labourers in various Parishes in this County, to attend Meetings, and to enter into Illegal Societies or Unions, to which they bind themselves by unlawful oaths, administered secretly by Persons concealed, who artfully deceive the ignorant and unwary,—WE, the undersigned Justices think it our duty to give this PUBLIC NOTICE and CAUTION, that all Persons may know the danger they incur by entering into such Societies.

ANY PERSON who shall become a Member of such a Society, or take any Oath, or assent to any Test or Declaration not authorized by Law—

Any Person who shall administer, or be present at, or consenting to the administering or taking any Unlawful Oath, or who shall cause such Oath to be administered, although not actually present at the time—

Any Person who shall not reveal or discover any Illegal Oath which may have been administered, or any Illegal Act done or to be done—

Any Person who shall induce, or endeavour to persuade any other Person to become a Member of such Societies,

WILL BECOME

Guilty of Felony,

AND BE LIABLE TO BE

Transported for Seven Years.

ANY PERSON who shall be compelled to take such an Oath, unless he shall declare the same within four days, together with the whole of what he shall know touching the same, will be liable to the same Penalty.

Any Person who shall directly or indirectly maintain correspondence or intercourse with such Society, will be deemed Guilty of an Unlawful Combination and Confederacy, and on Conviction before one Justice, on the Oath of one Witness, be liable to a Penalty of TWENTY POUNDS, or to be committed to the Common Gaol or House of Correction, for THREE CALENDAR MONTHS; or if proceeded against by Indictment, may be CONVICTED OF FELONY, and be TRANSPORTED FOR SEVEN YEARS.

Any Person who shall knowingly permit any Meeting of any such Society to be held in any House, Building, or other Place, shall for the first offence be liable to the Penalty of FIVE POUNDS; and for every other offence committed after Conviction, be deemed Guilty of such Unlawful Combination and Confederacy, and on Conviction before one Justice, on the Oath of one Witness, be liable to a Penalty of TWENTY POUNDS, or to Commitment in the Common Gaol or House of Correction, FOR THREE CALENDAR MONTHS; or if proceeded against by Indictment may be

CONVICTED OF FELONY,
And Transported for SEVEN YEARS.

COUNTY OF DORSET,
Dorchester Division

February 22d. 1834.

C. B. WOLLASTON,
JAMES FRAMPTON,
WILLIAM ENGLAND,
THOS. DADE,
JNO. MORTON COLSON,

HENRY FRAMPTON,
RICHD. TUCKER STEWARD,
WILLIAM R. CHURCHILL,
AUGUSTUS FOSTER.

17 An engraving (1836) to commemorate a meeting of trade unionists at Copenhagen Fields in of the late nineteenth century were far more extensive than those of the period 1750–1830.

per week to only 7s. The magistrates did this, and announced that for the year after this the wages would be lowered to only 6s. per week. The already starving labourers were to be squeezed even further. Some of the Tolpuddle farm labourers

April 1834. London had not yet spread out this far—a reminder that the industrial and social changes

were not willing to accept this. George Loveless sent for two members of a trade society who came to show the workers how to form a branch of the Grand National Consolidated Trade Union in Tolpuddle.

18 A contemporary drawing of the five 'martyrs' who returned to England on their release from gaol in Tasmania.

News of the formation of the branch was leaked by an informer to the magistrates, the warning notice was posted on 21 February, 1834 and on 24 February the six founders of the branch were arrested.

They were brought for trial before the local magistrates. The account of the trial makes it clear that the men had done nothing illegal—for this reason they were later to be pardoned. However the magistrates, with the very active support and advice of Lord Melbourne, were determined to stop the spread of this 'new disease'. They unearthed an Act of 1797 (the year of the naval mutinies) which forbade the taking of illegal oaths; they decided that the oath of initiation was an illegal oath (which was not true, otherwise the men would hardly have received their free pardon later on), and sentenced the 'culprits' to seven years' transportation to Tasmania.

This might have been the end of the matter if it had not been for the activity of the G.N.C.T.U. and other unions, who gained the support of Radical MPs and writers. In 1834 the leaders of the G.N.C.T.U. organised mammoth demonstrations against the Whigs and demanded the release and pardon of the Tolpuddle unionists. The most famous demonstration was that which ended in a mass meeting at Copenhagen Fields (near the present site of King's Cross Station). Over 100,000 union members are said to have attended the meeting, which was 'impressive, orderly and peaceful'.

The government at first ignored these protests from Owen and his Union, and the power which Owen had hoped to exercise (to create a New Moral Order) was seen to be non-existent—he could not even force the government to put right a very obvious wrong. How then could he hope to change the structure of society, a much more difficult task? This was one of the reasons for the failure of Owen's Union.

However, Radical MPs and writers continued to harry the Whig government; lawyers protested at the unfair trial, union leaders protested at the use of the Mutiny Act as the basis of condemning union leaders. Finally in 1836 the govern-

19 A committee of MPs and union leaders campaigned for two years for the release of the 'martyrs'. In April 1836 they held a dinner to celebrate their success.

CAUSE OF FREEDOM!

The LONDON CENTRAL DORCHESTER COMMITTEE feel great pleasure in informing their Fellow-Workmen and all Enemies to Oppression, that a

PUBLIC DINNER

WILL TAKE PLACE AT

WHITE CONDUIT HOUSE,

ON

Monday, April 25, 1836,

IN

CELEBRATION OF THE REMISSION OF THE SENTENCE

ON THE

DORCHESTER LABOURERS,

And in Commemoration of the Moral Power displayed by the Working Classes of London in their great Procession, April, 1834.

T. WAKLEY, ESQ. M.P.

WILL PRESIDE.

COMMITTEE OF MANAGEMENT.

Messrs. T. BAKER.   J. BROWN.   W. ISAACS.   G. TOMEY.   J. RICHES.   T. PEAK.

LONDON DORCHESTER CENTRAL COMMITTEE.

Mr. W. ISAACS, 7, Saffron Street, Saffron Hill
— T. BAKER, Young's Coffee House, 77, Curtain Rd.
— G. TOMEY, 33, Little Russell Street, Bloomsbury
— J. RICHES, 11, Marmaduke Court, John Street, St. George's East
— J. DAY, 1, Linton's Place, Limehouse Lock
— J. WHARTNABY, 61, John St., Blackfriars Road
— WINN, 11, Hatfield Place, Cross Street, Broadwall
— WALKER, 6, Marlborough Street, New Cut
— BURKINYOUNG, 2, Richmond Place, East Lane, Walworth
— BROWN, 91, Leather Lane
— BARNES, 1, Collingwood Street, Camberwell

Mr. PRICE, 2, Bath Place, Portland Street, Walworth
— SIMPSON, Elm Cottage, Waterloo Street, Camberwell
— PHILLIPS, Cock, Camberwell
— WENLOCK, Horse and Groom, Gresse Street, Rathbone Place
— GARDINER, 5, Petty's Ct., Hanway, St., Oxford St.
— T. PEAK, 8, James Street, Stepney
— R. LOVELESS, 48, Paddington St., Marylebone
— BUSH, 9, Church Street, Kennington
— LAKE, 1, Bedford Street, Walworth
— R. HARTWELL, (*Secretary*), 35, Brooke Street, West Square, Lambeth.

STEWARDS.

Mr. W. D. SAULL, (*Treasurer*), 15, Aldersgate Street
Rev. Dr. WADE, 8, Trellick Terrace, Pimlico
Mr. A. H. BEAUMONT, 24, Brompton Square
— J. ROBERTS BLACK, M.D., Chelsea
— W. HOARE, 1, Somers Place, New Road
— G. SIMKINS, 9, Stephen St., Tottenham Court Rd.
— G. NORMAN, ditto
— HAYNES, 4, Princes Street, Stepney Green
— WILKINSON, 28, Trafalgar Street, Walworth

Mr. PARTRIDGE, 8, Summers Street, Clerkenwell
— JOHN BELL, New True Sun Office, Bride Lane
— PETERS, White Conduit House
— HAMILTON, 4, West Street, Globe Fields
— WOOSTER, 31, Ashford Street, Hoxton
— J. ROBERTS, 25, Robert Street, Hampstead Road
— TAPSON, 17, Clifton Street North, Finsbury
— TALBOT, 9, Bedford St., Commercial Road (East)

Tickets 2s. 6d. each.—Double Tickets {To admit a Lady and Gentleman} 4s. 6d.

Tickets may be obtained of the Stewards and Committee as above; at the Committee Room, Turk's Head, King Street, Holborn; at the Bar of White Conduit House; and at the following places:

RISING SUN, East Lane, Walworth
ROSE AND CROWN, Colville Court Charlotte Street, Fitzroy Square
PRESSLEY'S COFFEE HOUSE, 69, John Street, Tottenham Court Road
LOVETT'S COFFEE HOUSE, 19, Greville Street, Hatton Garden
MECHANICS' INSTITUTION TAVERN, Circus Street, New Road

DUKE OF WELLINGTON, High Street, Shoreditch
FOX AND GOOSE, Bermondsey Street
STAR COFFEE HOUSE, William Street Hampstead Road
WESTMINSTER LITERARY INSTITUTION, Grosvenor Street, Milbank
Mr. WATSON, Publisher, 18, Commercial Place, City Road

DINNER ON TABLE AT HALF-PAST TWO PRECISELY.
In the course of the Afternoon several appropriate Glees will be sung.

The whole arrangements of the day will be under the immediate superintendence of the London Dorchester Central Committee, who pledge themselves that nothing shall be wanting on their part to ensure the comfort and convenience of those who may assemble to celebrate the day; and they feel confident that their exertions will be ably seconded by Mr. Peters, the landlord. The Dinner will be served hot, of the best description, in the large Room of the Tavern, and will consist of every sort of Roast and Boiled Meats, Hams, Vegetables, Bread, Porter; Plumb Pudding, and Tarts.

The Committee of Management meet every Wednesday, at the Turk's Head, King Street, Holborn; also on Monday and Saturday evenings, April 18 and 23, to issue Tickets and receive Money for those sold.

20 Plug Riots at Preston, August 1842. Violence was still a common feature of life as Chartists riots at Newport and incidents like this one at Preston illustrate.

ment agreed to pardon the 'culprits'. The prisoners in Tasmania were not told of their good fortune; it was by sheer chance that George Loveless read of it in a newspaper that came out to Tasmania. The London Dorchester Committee of union leaders and MPs collected money to bring them home and set them up in life again in England, in 1838.

The Tolpuddle affair was not the only reason for the failure of Robert Owen's scheme. From the beginning the four largest unions in the country never joined—the builders, the potters, the spinners and the clothiers. Owen's Union never had enough funds to support those who went on strike or were locked out by the employers. This meant that the men suffered great hardship during their strike and were finally forced to return to work on the conditions laid down by the masters. It was small wonder that the workers were soon convinced that the G.N.C.T.U. could do nothing for them.

Often the local secretaries or treasurers of the Union handled large sums of money—contributions from members, or strike pay sent out by the London executive. These local officials were working men who themselves received the usual poor wage of their fellow workers. It is not surprising that very often they made off with the funds.

Owen, like so many other Radical and liberal theorists and writers, made the mistake of thinking that all the workers shared only a common bond and had no different interests. He soon found out that turners in Plymouth felt little loyalty for turners in Glasgow, while spinners in Lancashire felt even less loyalty for carpenters in Yorkshire. This lack of working class unity was made worse by the inadequate system of communications, which also hampered the activities of the G.N.C.T.U. leaders.

Owen himself antagonised very many Union members. His atheism offended some, his socialism offended others; his utopian dreams offended the practical working men while it also brought down the severity of the law on everyone connected with trade unionism. By the autumn of 1834 his scheme for a strike-inspired New Moral Order had foundered in the magistrates court at Tolpuddle.

Owen himself turned to other schemes. Many union members gave their free time, money and support to more practical ways of improving their conditions. Some turned to the Factory Reform Movement; others turned back to the formation and strengthening of small, local, craft unions. Many were to support the Anti-Corn Law League; the dreamers and visionaries saw Chartism as the road to the new society.

Further Reading
M. Cole: *Robert Owen of New Lanark (1771–1858)* (Batchworth)
S. and B. Webb: *History of Trade Unionism* (Longmans)
H. Pelling: *History of British Trade Unionism* (Macmillan)

3 Model Unions, 1851–1880

Unions for the Skilled Worker

The over-ambitious Grand National Unions aimed at changing the social structure of Britain largely through the medium of the General Strike. Government, judges and magistrates and employers had reacted strongly against this plan. The men who now took the lead in trade union development had more limited aims; without violence, with as few strikes as was possible, these leaders worked to improve the conditions of their members within the existing social system.

National craft unions were founded in the 1850s and 1860s for joiners, boilermakers, bricklayers and shoemakers. But the most famous of these 'Model Unions' was the Amalgamated Society of Engineers (which helped to form the Amalgamated Engineering Union in 1920). This union, as its title shows, was an amalgamation of a number of small, often local, unions, all of whose members were highly skilled craftsmen.

These unions were founded at a time when Britain's economy was booming. The rapid development of the British railway system was creating employment in many industries. Skilled craftsmen could earn high wages in this period and employment was regular.

At the same time, the Free Trade policy begun by Sir Robert Peel (1841–46), and carried on by William Gladstone as Chancellor of the Exchequer, led to a continual fall in the price of imports, particularly food. The skilled craftsman's high wages bought more as prices fell; he and his family began to buy goods which had been luxuries, such as meat, sugar and butter, bought more and better

21 The 'opening of the first English rail-way between Stockton and Darlington, Sept. 27th, 1825'. were 6,000 miles of railway line in Britain.

22 The prosperous-looking, well-dressed wives of the skilled workers enjoy themselves at a picnic in the Shirley Hills. No ragged clothes or pinched cheeks here.

clothes, used the new railways for excursions to the seaside. Thousands of workers began to have enough money to save, as is shown by the growth in the number of Post Office Savings accounts.

These craftsmen could afford the high fees charged by their unions, often as much as 1s. 6d. a week. Part of this fee was used by the union to provide friendly society benefits to members; the sick, unemployed, retired or injured union member would not become destitute, nor would he have to join the ranks of 'the poor'.

Part of the fee was used to pay full-time union officials, one of whose tasks was

Railway transport, however, was not fully developed until the late 1830s and 1840s. By 1850 there

23 Robert Applegarth, William Allen and George Odger.

to negotiate with employers. Many employers soon recognised the value of such negotiations, which fixed wage rates, working conditions and hours. The sober, practical, moderate union leaders were anxious to make the negotiations a success —they did not want to waste their union funds in strike-pay; they were also anxious to make sure that their members carried out the agreements once these were made—otherwise employers would not pay so much attention to the union leaders in the future.

The leaders of the Model Unions made London their headquarters. London was the centre of the railway network, it was also the seat of government where the union leaders hoped to influence politicians. If they could show the country's rulers that the Model Unions were not revolutionary or violent they hoped that they could persuade the politicians to change the laws affecting trade unionism.

Five national, craft, Model Unions made their headquarters in London. The leaders of these unions frequently met, soon formed the London Trades Council, and worked together as delegates to the politicians and press. Beatrice Webb later called this group 'the Junta'. They tried to influence trade union development throughout the whole country, where most unions were still local, many were less moderate than the Junta and where not all employers were convinced of the value of organised workers.

In many towns and villages the various local unions formed trades councils to which each union sent delegates. Some of these councils accepted the advice and leadership of the Junta. Many were more militant, coming under the influence of Owen's ideas. These militants were against the rather cautious policy of the Junta; they wanted more action and greater change.

The clash between employers, unwilling to accept trade unions, and workers, anxious to have such an organisation, frequently became violent. Employers locked out would-be unionists, replaced their labour with workers brought in from other parts of the country. The strikers often attacked this 'blackleg' labour and tried to prevent the new workers from entering the factory, mine or workshop. The magistrates and the police tended to side with the employers, and clashes between police and workers were frequent.

These conflicts reached a climax in 1866 when a strike by file-grinders in Sheffield led to gunpowder attacks on factories and employers' houses; one bomb attack on the home of a non-striking workman led to two deaths. These 'Sheffield outrages' led to public demand for an investigation not only into the incidents at Sheffield, but into trade unionism in general. Newspapers accused the whole union movement of being involved in the incidents. This led the trade unionists to ask for a Commission of Inquiry into the Sheffield outrages. This Commission was appointed in May 1867.

24 Police protection was often required when employers brought workers from other areas or countries to take the place of strikers. This drawing from the *Illustrated London News* (September 1871) shows the anger of Newcastle engineers at the arrival of foreign workers.

PROPOSED CONGRESS OF TRADES COUNCILS

AND OTHER

Federations of Trades Societies.

MANCHESTER, FEBRUARY 21st, 1868.

FELLOW-UNIONISTS,

The Manchester and Salford Trades Council having recently taken into their serious consideration the present aspect of Trades Unions, and the profound ignorance which prevails in the public mind with reference to their operations and principles, together with the probability of an attempt being made by the Legislature, during the present session of Parliament, to introduce a measure detrimental to the interests of such Societies, beg most respectfully to suggest the propriety of holding in Manchester, as the main centre of industry in the provinces, a Congress of the Representatives of Trades Councils and other similar Federations of Trades Societies. By confining the Congress to such bodies it is conceived that a deal of expense will be saved, as Trades will thus be represented collectively; whilst there will be a better opportunity afforded of selecting the most intelligent and efficient exponents of our principles.

It is proposed that the Congress shall assume the character of the annual meetings of the British Association for the Advancement of Science and the Social Science Association, in the transactions of which Societies the artizan class are almost entirely excluded; and that papers, previously carefully prepared, shall be laid before the Congress on the various subjects which at the present time affect Trades Societies, each paper to be followed by discussion upon the points advanced, with a view of the merits and demerits of each question being thoroughly ventilated through the medium of the public press. It is further suggested that the subjects treated upon shall include the following:—

1.—Trades Unions an absolute necessity.
2.—Trades Unions and Political Economy.
3.—The Effect of Trades Unions on Foreign Competition.
4.—Regulation of the Hours of Labour.
5.—Limitation of Apprentices.
6.—Technical Education.
7.—Arbitration and Courts of Conciliation.
8.—Co-operation.
9.—The present Inequality of the Law in regard to Conspiracy, Intimidation, Picketing, Coercion, &c.
10.—Factory Acts Extension Bill, 1867: the necessity of Compulsory Inspection, and its application to all places where Women and Children are employed.
11.—The present Royal Commission on Trades Unions: how far worthy of the confidence of the Trades Union interest.
12.—The necessity of an Annual Congress of Trade Representatives from the various centres of industry.

All Trades Councils and other Federations of Trades are respectfully solicited to intimate their adhesion to this project on or before the 6th of April next, together with a notification of the subject of the paper that each body will undertake to prepare; after which date all information as to place of meeting, &c., will be supplied.

It is also proposed that the Congress be held on the 4th of May next, and that all liabilities in connection therewith shall not extend beyond its sittings.

Communications to be addressed to MR. W. H. WOOD, Typographical Institute, 29, Water Street, Manchester.

By order of the Manchester and Salford Trades Council,

S. C. NICHOLSON, PRESIDENT.
W. H. WOOD, SECRETARY.

26 Beaconsfield Buildings at Stroud Vale, Islington, provided homes for the prosperous workers.

Legislation

At the same time the legal position of trade unions was endangered as a result of a law case. A local official of the Boilermakers Union had absconded with union funds. When the Union prosecuted him the judge ruled that trade unions were not legal bodies and so could not bring a case. He agreed that any individual member of the union could bring a case and could recover his small share of the stolen funds. In view of the expense involved this was not worthwhile and the dishonest official escaped punishment. This was another reason why the trade unionists wanted a Commission of Inquiry into the movement as a whole.

In February 1867, before the Sheffield Commission was appointed, the government had set up a Royal Commission of Inquiry into Trade Unions. The Junta or London Trades Council, gave evidence to this Commission. So also did delegates from other local trades councils. Two different voices spoke for the union movement. Samuel Nicholson and William Wood, then President and Secretary of the Manchester and Salford Trades Council, hoped that the movement might learn to speak with one voice. In February 1868 they sent out invitations to all trades councils to a Trade Union Congress to be held in Manchester in June 1868. The London Trades Council and the Junta did not attend this Congress;

they saw it as a rival to their own hard-won position of power. The first Trade Union Congress was, therefore, held without them.

Meanwhile the Royal Commission had published its findings. It declared that where trade unions were properly organised there was little danger of violence, and few, if any, strikes. The Commission praised the Junta-type union with its friendly society benefits, practice of negotiations and control over its members.

The government, led by Gladstone, then passed two Acts affecting trade unions. The Trade Union Act, 1871, said that unions were now legal bodies; this safeguarded their funds. However, the Criminal Law Amendment Act, 1871, while allowing unions the right to strike, made picketing illegal.

The trade union movement campaigned to have this last law changed. Union leaders worked for the fall of the Gladstone government in 1874 and for the return of the Conservatives under Disraeli, who, in 1875, repealed the Amendment Act.

By 1875 the legal basis of trade unions seemed secure. But now Germany, France and the United States were beginning to challenge Britain's industrial supremacy. Although the golden age of British industry was ending, highly paid skilled craftsmen continued to lead lives of luxury compared to those of the mass of the working people.

Further Reading
Pattison: *Trade Union History* (Barrie and Rockliffe)
A. Hutt: *British Trade Unionism, 1800–1961* (Lawrence & Wishart)
Robertson: *The Trade Unions* (Hamish Hamilton)

4 Unions for Unskilled Workers, 1880–1910

Conditions for the Unskilled Worker

This prosperity was not shared by the unskilled workers. These continued to work long hours for little money; for them unemployment and the workhouse were never far away. Poorly paid, they had no savings to fall back on; they could not afford the luxury of new terraced housing in the suburbs; they counted a room in a slum as home. Their children went on excursions only when charity provided; far from acquiring more possessions they were often forced to pawn the few they had in order to get enough money to continue to exist.

27 Close number 193, High Street, Glasgow, in 1868. Millions of unskilled workers lived in slums such as these.

28 A voluntary society, the Bethnal Green Employment Association, tried to provide some paid work for the unemployed in this Labour Yard. This drawing (1868) shows the hopelessness of life for many unskilled workers.

Some of them were employed in the docks, gasworks and factories. Many worked in uninspected workshops or at home in the 'sweated industries'. None of these jobs required any great skill; some called for physical strength, some for deft fingers. There was always a plentiful supply of men and women capable of doing their jobs, eager to pick up even the poor pay as the only alternative to the workhouse.

The skilled workers tended to 'look down' on the labouring poor. Until the late 1880s no one had thought of creating unions for them. However in 1888 Annie Besant helped to organise a union of girls working in the match factory of

29 Members of the matchmakers' union, 1888.

30 How many of these will the foreman choose today? What will happen to the others and to their families?

Bryant and Mays. Here for 2d. an hour, girls dipped matches into phosphorus, an occupation which often led to a terrible disease known as 'phossy jaw', caused by the fumes from the phosphorus. It could be fatal but even if a worker recovered she might lose the whole of her lower jaw.

These unskilled women workers won their case for better pay after a strike. In August 1889 Will Thorne organised the employees of the London gasworks. These men did a physically hard job. Thorne and the Gas Workers Union demanded an eight-hour day instead of the existing 12 hours. The employers gave way before the threat of a strike.

The most famous unskilled union was that formed in the London Docks. Employment on the docks was a haphazard affair; men waited for work until the tide, weather conditions and the presence of a ship combined to provide some —for a few. The representative of the shipping company (**30**) can be seen picking out the few men he needs for the work in hand. The rest would have to wait—in vain perhaps—for the rest of the day. Even those chosen might work for only an hour or so. Their wage was 5d. an hour.

The Dock Strike, 1889

Ben Tillett had had a hand in the forming of the Gas Workers Union. During this time he had met John Burns and Tom Mann, members of the Amalgamated Society of Engineers, who were anxious to spread the idea of unionism among the unskilled workers. Tillett organised a Tea Workers' and General Labourers' Union which, in August 1889, demanded that no docker should be taken on for less than four hours and that wages should be 6d. an hour with 8d. an hour for overtime.

SOUTH SIDE CENTRAL STRIKE COMMITTEE,
SAYES COURT, DEPTFORD.
SEPTEMBER 10, 1889.

GENERAL MANIFESTO.

Owing to the fact that the demands of the Corn Porters, Deal Porters, Granary Men, General Steam Navigation Men, Permanent Men and General Labourers on the South Side have been misrepresented, the above Committee have decided to issue this Manifesto, stating the demands of the various sections now on Strike, and pledge themselves to support each section in obtaining their demands.

DEAL PORTERS of the Surrey Commercial Docks have already placed their demands before the Directors.

LUMPERS (Outside) demand the following Rates, viz:— 1. 10d. per standard for Deals. 2. 11d. per stand. for all Goods rating from 2 x 4 to 2½ x 7, or for rough boards. 3. 1s. per std. for plain boards. Working day from 7 a.m. to 5 p.m., and that no man leave the "Red Lion" corner before 6.45 a.m. Overtime at the rate of 6d. per hour extra from 5 p.m. including meal times.

STEVEDORES (Inside) demand 8d. per hour from 7 a.m. to 5 p.m. 1s. per hour overtime. Overtime to commence from 5 p.m. to 7 a.m. Pay to commence from leaving "Red Lion" corner. Meal times to be paid for. Holidays & Meal times double pay, and that the Rules of the United Stevedores Protection League be acceded to in every particular. *Conceded*

OVERSIDE CORN PORTERS (S.C.D.) demand 15s.3d. per 100 qrs. for Oats. Heavy labour 17s.4d. per 100 qrs. manual, or with use of Steam 16s.1d. All overtime after 6 p.m. to be paid at the rate of ½d. per qr. extra.

QUAY CORN PORTERS (S. C. D.) demand the return of Standard prices previous to March 1889, which had been in operation for 17 years.

TRIMMERS AND GENERAL LABOURERS demand 6d. per hour from 7 a.m. to 6 p.m. and 8d. per hour Overtime; Meal times as usual; and not to be taken on for less than 4 hours.

WEIGHERS & WAREHOUSEMEN demand to be reinstated in their former positions without distinction.

BERMONDSEY AND ROTHERHITHE WALL CORN PORTERS demand: 1. Permanent Men 30s. per week. 2. Casual Men 5s. 10d. per day and 8d. per hour Overtime; Overtime to commence at 6 p.m. Meal times as usual.

GENERAL STEAM NAVIGATION MEN demand:—1. Wharf Men, 6d. per hour from 6 a.m. to 6 p.m. and 8d. per hour Overtime. 2. In the Stream, 7d. per hour ordinary time, 9d. per hour Overtime. 3. In the Dock, 8d. per hour ordinary time, 1s. per hour Overtime.

MAUDSLEY'S ENGINEER'S MEN. Those receiving 21s. per week now demand 24s., and those receiving 24s. per week demand 26s.

ASHBY'S, LTD., CEMENT WORKS demand 6d. per ton landing Coals and Chalk. General Labourers 10% rise of wages all round, this making up for a reduction made 3 years ago.

GENERAL LABOURERS, TELEGRAPH CONSTRUCTION demand 4s. per day from 6 a.m. to 5 p.m., time and a quarter for first 2 hours Overtime, and if later, time and a half for all Overtime. No work to be done in Meal Hours.

Signed on behalf of the Central Committee, Wade Arms,
BEN. TILLETT,
JOHN BURNS,
TOM MANN,
H. H. CHAMPION,
JAS. TOOMEY.

Signed on behalf of the South side Committee,
JAS. SULLY
CHAS. H
HUGH J

...side to be sent to Mr HUGH BRO...   ...Central Strike Committee, Sayes Court.

31 The Manifesto of the dockers showed how many unions were involved in the London Docks Strike and the objects for which each was striking.

32 The dockers marched through London, 1889. Notice the floats which illustrated the nature of the work done at the Docks.

Tillett's union had no funds and little organisation but to most people's surprise it won the support of the other dock workers in many other trades. All of them came out on strike in sympathy with the General Labourers. The Manifesto (**31**) shows the nature and extent of their demands.

John Burns stage-managed a series of marches through London (**32**). These gained a good deal of sympathy from a public which had not known how poorly paid the dockers were.

For five weeks London's docks were at a standstill. Finally the employers agreed to see a Mediation Committee at the Lord Mayor's Mansion House. Here, under the chairmanship of Cardinal Manning, an agreement was reached on 15 September, 1889. The dockers were to get 6d. an hour. More important, the Dock, Wharf, Riverside and General Labourers Union was formed with Tillett as its full-time secretary.

These new unions were more militant than the moderate, cautious leaders of the craft unions. They had little to offer employers in negotiations; their main weapon was the strike. These new organisations were also poorer than the craft unions. Their members could not afford the high fees charged by the older unions; Tillett's General Labourers only paid 2d. a week, which did not enable the Union to offer friendly society benefits to its members.

The skilled worker with his high wages enjoyed a different life from that led by the poorly paid labourer. The difference was shown in many ways. The unskilled labourer, even when backed by a union, could never earn enough to afford good housing; his union would never make payments to him in time of sickness, unemployment or old age.

The Trade Unions and Socialism

Henry Hyndman, a London stockbroker, was one of the few Englishmen to have read Karl Marx's *Das Kapital* which had been written in 1867. In 1881 Hyndman founded the Social Democratic Federation whose members were mainly middle class, and which called for a socialist programme of reform. One of his early followers, William Morris, broke away to form the Socialist League. In 1884 another middle class group, including the Webbs, H. George Wells and Bernard Shaw, formed the Fabian Society. The Fabians hoped that they could persuade the existing political parties to adopt a socialist programme.

33 Violence during a strike. Here, at the Railway Bridge, Motherwell, railway strikers clash with the police and soldiers (1891).

34 The matchbox maker. The matchboxes (filled) retailed for 2d. a dozen. She made 2d. a gross and worked 12 hours a day for less than 5s. weekly.

These movements were a reaction by the middle class to the shocking conditions in which the majority of the working class lived and worked. The socialists believed that the country was wealthy enough to afford reforms which would raise the standard of living of the masses.

Henry George, an American writer, published *Progress and Poverty* in 1879. A best seller, it made socialist ideas known to the leaders of the working classes, like Burns, Tillett and Mann.

The old craft unions had supported the Liberal Party. A number of working men had been elected to Parliament as Lib-Labs—they sat and voted with the Liberals. The leaders of the new unions, however, were easily converted to socialism. Only through state action could the labouring poor hope to improve their standards of living. Neither the Liberal nor the Conservative parties showed any inclination to carry out a programme of social reform. Burns, Tillett and Mann had demonstrated that working class industrial action could improve conditions. At the Trade Union Congress in 1887, Keir Hardie, representing the Scottish miners, asked that the workers should form their own political party. The T.U.C., still dominated by the skilled unions, rejected the demand. In 1889, the year of the London Docks strike, Scottish working men formed their own Independent Labour Party. By 1892 this movement had spread to England, and Burns, Hardie and Havelock Wilson (the seamen's union leader), were elected to Parliament. To symbolise that this was the beginning of a new age, Hardie arrived at the House of Commons wearing a cloth cap and accompanied by a brass band. He was as unwelcome in the Commons as he was in the T.U.C.

In 1893 the Fabians realised that they had failed to get their ideas adopted by either of the two main parties. Bernard Shaw wrote a famous article, *To your tents O Israel*, which called upon the working class to support the formation of a Labour party. Shaw argued that only with the support of union organisation and funds could such a party succeed.

35 This picture of a pawnshop at Merthyr Tydfil, 1875, shows the lower-paid workers waiting to pawn their few possessions to get money for food and rent. A sign of the improvement in the standard of living over the last 30 years has been the disappearance of the pawnshop.

In 1893 the leaders of the various socialist societies met at Bradford under the chairmanship of Keir Hardie and formed the Independent Labour Party. Although the T.U.C. refused to support the new party, many of the younger leaders of the unions were disposed to support it. One of these, G. N. Barnes, became general secretary of the A.S.E. in 1896.

Partly owing to the converts in the older unions and partly owing to the increasing number of unskilled unions at the T.U.C., in 1899 the T.U.C. carried a resolution advocating a conference of delegates from the socialist societies, co-operative organisations and trade unions. This conference met in London in 1900. The trade union delegates represented only 2/5 of the workers affiliated to the T.U.C. since the majority of unions were still not convinced that the formation of a Labour party was necessary.

The London conference established the Labour Representation Committee, which quickly became known as the Labour Party even though this name was not adopted until 1906.

The skilled unions were soon driven to support the new party. Increasing foreign competition led to regular unemployment in Britain's older industries. Employers, anxious to sell their products, tried to force down wages, and from 1900 to 1914 the standard of living of the skilled worker did not rise as it had done for so long. In many cases it fell, as unemployment and falling wages lowered family incomes. Reluctantly some members of skilled unions began to think that state action might be necessary to improve their living standards.

But above all it was the Taff Vale verdict which was decisive. A strike had taken place on the Taff Vale railway in South Wales. The company had lost money as a result of the strike and sued the Amalgamated Society of Railway Servants for damages. In 1901 the company was awarded £23,000 damages and the Union ordered to pay, in addition, £19,000 in legal costs. This decision was a new danger for the unions, since, even if a strike were successful, their funds might be taken away by claims for damages.

Only Parliament could alter this state of affairs, but neither the Conservative

36 Keir Hardie speaking in Trafalgar Square, May 1913. His Labour Party had grown steadily and was then represented in Parliament by 42 MPs.

37 A young striker addresses some of the thousand girls on strike at Morton, Motherwell, 18 March, 1914. Women became more aggressive, seeking not only political equality with men, but also something approaching economic equality.

government nor the Liberal opposition showed any inclination to propose legislation to safeguard union funds. The unions were, almost against their will, driven to support the infant Labour Party. In 1906 the Party put forward 50 candidates, 29 of whom were elected; 23 of these were trade union representatives. There were also 14 Lib-Lab MPs, representing the older tradition of union voting, and 12 MPs sponsored by the Miners' Union. These joined the Labour Party in 1909.

This much larger, widely supported party voted with the Liberal government (1906–14), particularly when it proposed legislation affecting the working classes. Above all it supported the Trades Dispute Act, 1906 which reversed the Taff Vale decision and safeguarded union funds from claims for damages arising from strikes.

When a trade union decided to support the Labour Party it used part of each member's weekly subscription as a 'political levy'. This money provided the funds for organisation of constituencies, for elections and above all to pay MPs who otherwise could not have afforded to give up their jobs. A railway worker, W. V. Osborne, secretary of the Walthamstow Branch of the A.S.R.S., was a Liberal. He objected to his union giving this financial support to the Labour Party. He prosecuted his union and the House of Lords decided in 1909 that the Trade Union Acts did not allow unions to use their funds for political purposes.

38 The lower-middle classes adopted trade unionism. These clerks had to wear masks to prevent their employers recognising and dismissing them. They were on their way to a rally in Hyde Park, September 1913.

The Labour Party was then faced with financial ruin. In part this was averted by the Parliament Act, 1911 which said that MPs were to receive a salary of £400 a year. Furthermore, the Trade Union Act, 1913, ruled that the political levy could be charged if the majority of union members agreed to it. Any member who objected to it was to be allowed to 'contract out' when he paid his weekly subscriptions.

The trade union movement had ceased to be a purely industrial body; it was now engaged in politics. It had also ceased to be an exclusive, skilled craftsmen's organisation. An increasing number of its workers belonged to the General Unions of unskilled workers and even the craft unions began to recruit members from among the semi-skilled and unskilled. Perhaps even more significant for the future was the formation of unions for the white-collar workers. Civil servants, journalists, Post Office workers, teachers and clerks were among those who formed trade unions. Trade unionism had spread down among the labouring poor; now it was reaching up into the lower-middle class.

Further Reading
A. Bullock: *The Life and Times of Ernest Bevin* (Heinemann)
E. H. P. Brown: *The Growth of British Industrial Relations* (Macmillan)
H. Pelling: *The Origins of the Labour Party, 1880–1900* (O.U.P.)

5 Industrial Unrest 1910–1914: The First World War

The period 1910–1914 was one of continued unrest in Britain. Women had been campaigning for equality for many years; now an extremist minority led by Mrs. Pankhurst took the lead in the agitation, which they publicised in various ways. Some women chained themselves to railings outside Buckingham Palace, the House of Commons and politicians' houses; others interrupted political meetings and even the proceedings of the House of Commons; one woman threw herself under the feet of King Edward VII's horse during the Derby.

This militant campaign was met by an equally militant reaction. Leading politicians denounced the campaign in strong language; their supporters attacked women hecklers; the police were far from gentle in their handling of suffragette demonstrators; judges passed harsh sentences on women found guilty of any mis-

39 Asquith led the attack on the power of the Lords (1910–12), arguing that the privileges of birth did not automatically entitle men to govern. Suffragettes thought him hypocritical to maintain, at the same time, that participation in government was the right of only one sex.

THE RIGHT DISHONOURABLE DOUBLE-FACE ASQUITH.

VOTES FOR WOMEN

Women's Social and Political Union.

4, Clement's Inn, London, W.C.

Citizen Asq—th: "Down with privilege of birth—up with Democratic rule!" | *Monseigneur Asq—th:* "The rights of government belong to the aristocrats by birth—men. No liberty or equality for women!"

behaviour. When women prisoners went on hunger-strike they were forcibly fed. Later the Cat-and-Mouse Act allowed the release of women prisoners on hunger-strike and their re-arrest when the authorities considered they had recovered enough strength to finish their sentence.

Newspapers carried stories of these activities from 1910 onwards. At the same time the House of Lords was involving the country in a constitutional crisis which plagued the last days of Edward VII's life and disturbed the first two years of the reign of the new King, George V. The Lords had rejected the 'People's Budget' introduced by Lloyd George in 1909. Some saw this as an attack on democracy by a handful of aristocratic peers; others saw the budget as an attempt to introduce socialism into Britain. The country had two elections in 1910 when the papers were full of reports of violent speeches by one side or the other. In 1911 the Parliament Bill was introduced to curb the powers of the House of Lords. When the Lords came to debate it there was grave danger that they would reject this measure, so plunging the country again into a 'Peers versus the People' campaign. Fortunately, wiser counsels prevailed; most of the Lords abstained in the final vote and the conflict subsided.

However, almost immediately Ireland became a menacing problem. The Liberal government passed a Home Rule Bill in 1912; this was rejected in the Lords but, as a result of the Parliament Act, 1911, it would automatically become law in 1914. So from 1912 onwards the Protestants of Ulster, aided by the majority of British Conservatives, prepared for civil war in 1914. Guns were brought from Germany, volunteers were enrolled in their thousands at emotional ceremonies, aristocratic houses were made ready to act as hospitals for the wounded. Meanwhile, the Liberal government prepared to use force to put down a rebellion in 1914.

This was the atmosphere of 1910–14. In the industrial world there was similar unrest. Continued foreign competition meant unemployment; wage rates did not keep pace with prices and standards of living fell. Union leaders, in common with the Lords and the women and Ulster Protestants, became more militant. The London dockers organised a big strike in 1911; so did dockers in Liverpool. In 1912 the Transport Workers Federation called a national strike, but this was a failure, leading to increased bitterness between union leaders and employers.

Syndicalism

The Transport Workers Federation was only one example of the spread of the doctrine of syndicalism. This aimed first at creating large industrial unions—one union for each industry. Then these unions would take control of the industry. This control might be won peacefully, according to the teachings of John Ruskin

40 Ben Tillett addresses strikers at Tower Hill, London, during the transport strike of 1912.

and William Morris who had founded the Guild Socialist movement in Britain. But most syndicalists realised that industrialists would not hand over control of their industries peacefully. They knew that militancy would be required. In 1910 Tillett had founded the Transport Workers Federation which called the unsuccessful strike of 1912. In 1912 the syndicalist-minded miners' union called a national coal strike. This involved 850,000 mineworkers and lasted for 5 weeks. In part this strike was a success, for the government intervened to pass the Coal Mines Act 1912 which guaranteed the miners a minimum wage. A. J. Cook and Noah Ablett, two of the miners' leaders, in *The Miners' Next Step*, called for even more militancy until the miners had won control of their industry.

In 1911 there was a two-day national railway strike which made people realise how much the country depended on the railway system. In 1912 three unions combined to form the National Union of Railwaymen, which by 1914 had doubled its membership. This seemed to be the first stage in a syndicalist approach to the problem of the railways.

Transport workers, miners and railwaymen had now formed large, militant unions. In 1913, Robert Smillie, the miners' leader, suggested that the three unions should act together in what came to be known as the 'Triple Alliance'. These unions represented nearly two million workers—a total far greater than anything Robert Owen had dreamed of.

Smillie's argument was that when one of these unions went on strike it created unemployment for members of the other unions. Thus in the coal strike of 1912 over 1,250,000 other workers were laid off owing to the shortage of coal. Similarly in the railway strike there was no coal shifted from the pitheads and miners were

41 Welsh miners being welcomed in Trafalgar Square by A. J. Cook, 1927.

42 During the First World War women were drawn into many spheres of work hitherto closed to them in order to free men for the army. It was feared that they would never go back to domestic service. If they could do men's work, why should they not have the vote?

laid off. Smillie suggested that all three unions should act together; they should present their demands to employers at the same time; if strikes were necessary all three unions should strike simultaneously.

The Triple Alliance seemed to be a major victory for the syndicalists. Through the threat of their triple-strike they would wield enormous power. No doubt the majority of their members thought of using this power only to improve working conditions and wages. A minority, however, hoped to achieve wider objectives including worker-control of industry.

Fortunately, or otherwise, the leaders of the Triple Alliance never organised a common leadership with the power to direct the activities of all three unions. Each union remained independent; the hope of the founders of the Alliance was that the leaders would always agree to support each other. However, as the events

43 John Hodge in 1931 when he was President of the British Steelworkers' Union. The power, respectability and sense of responsibility of twentieth-century trade unionism were all illustrated by his position in Lloyd George's cabinet in 1916.

of the 1920s were to show, joint action could not be achieved while each union remained independent.

The Trade Unionists in Wartime

The coming of the war in 1914 ended all the unrest; Ireland was forgotten by all save a minority of Sinn Feiners; women gave up direct action and took up war work; the Conservatives, who had so bitterly opposed Lloyd George, were to be his main supporters when he became Prime Minister in 1916. And all except a handful of militant unionists gave up their aggressive attitude.

The war was, almost surprisingly, an important period in the development of the trade union movement. Unions showed their patriotism by giving up many of their privileges, principally the right to strike—for the duration of the war they agreed to submit all disputes to arbitration. They also agreed to allow unskilled labour, including women, to do work that had previously been done only by skilled workers. This 'dilution' was especially important in the engineering and munitions industries.

Trade unionists also learned to play a part in the government of the country. Lloyd George realised the importance of getting the support of the working class. He was the first minister ever to address the T.U.C.—he did so as Minister for Munitions in 1915. When he became Prime Minister in 1916 he created a Ministry of Labour and made the Secretary of the Steel Smelters, John Hodge, the first Minister; at the same time he made the secretary of the Amalgamated Society of Engineers, G. N. Barnes, the Minister for Pensions. He quickly agreed to the T.U.C.'s suggestion for state control of the mines, shipping and the distribution of food.

Many thousands of trade unionists were involved in the more than 2,000 national and local advisory committees that were set up to further the war effort. This experience of 'having a seat in the cab' was important in developing the trade unions' own self-respect and other people's esteem for the loyalty and ability of trade unionists.

The employment of thousands of women workers and regular employment for the mass of male workers led to a rise in family incomes. Many people enjoyed a high standard of living in spite of the increase in prices during the war. After the war, trade unionists, now more experienced, were unwilling to accept cuts in their living standards. In this sense the war may be seen as an extra cause of the industrial unrest which came when peace 'broke out' in 1918.

Further Reading
B. Tillett: *Memories and Reflections* (Longs)
R. Page: *The Miners: Year of Struggle* (Allen & Unwin)
G. Dangerfield: *The Strange Death of Liberal England* (MacGibbon & Kee)

6 From the First World War to the General Strike

Post-war Boom and Depression

In 1916 Harry Gosling, the President of the T.U.C., said '... we hope for something better than a mere avoidance of unemployment and strikes after the war'. From 1918 until the spring of 1920 his hopes were more than realised. There was a great post-war demand for goods and machinery, and the country enjoyed a period of high wages and full employment.

This encouraged the more militant trade unionists. In September 1919 the railwaymen, led by J. H. Thomas, went on strike against the government's attempt

44 *(left)* Harry Gosling, optimistic president of the T.U.C. in 1916. **45** *(right)* The Dockers' K.C., Ernest Bevin, in 1920.

46 During the coal strike of 1921, the miner's wife takes the familiar path to the pawnshop.

to lower their minimum wage from 51s. to 40s. a week. On 5 October the government agreed to postpone the reduction for at least a year. In March 1920 the miners, still led by Robert Smillie, won an increase in pay from the Lloyd George Coalition government. Early in 1920 Ernest Bevin won the title of the Dockers' K.C. because of the way he presented evidence before a Commission of Inquiry. This Commission, largely as a result of Bevin's work, awarded higher wages to the dockers.

All three members of the Triple Alliance had won battles.

In the spring of 1920 the post-war boom came to an end. Britain's share of world trade fell as Japan, Germany and the United States became more vigorous competitors. Britain continued to produce goods of which the world wanted less. She failed to develop newer industries as quickly as her rivals.

By early 1921 over 2,000,000 men were unemployed—22% of the insured workers of the country, compared with an annual average of about 6% during the years before 1914. The average level of unemployment from 1922 to 1929 was about 10% of all insured workers, but some areas had a much higher level than others. Clydeside, Tyneside, Lancashire and South Wales became depressed areas as the older industries of coal, iron, shipbuilding and cotton textiles found it harder to sell their goods.

The coal industry was particularly hard hit. British coal was more expensive than coal from modern, mechanised German, Polish and American mines. And world demand for coal was falling as oil and electricity were more and more used.

The government had taken over the running of the mines during the war. While these were making a post-war profit the government continued this control. But in February 1921 the government announced that it would hand the mines back to their private owners on 31 March. The owners declared that they could not agree to continue the 1920 wage agreements, made while the boom was on. They announced that substantial wage cuts would be required. The miners' leaders refused to accept a reduction in wages, so a coal strike began on 1 April, 1921.

The miners now called on the other members of the Triple Alliance for support, and a general strike was announced for 15 April. The transport workers and railwaymen were, obviously, not fighting the mine-owners; their threat of a strike was intended to force the government to intervene in the industry. Lloyd George agreed to negotiate with the leaders of the three unions, J. H. Thomas for the railwaymen, Ernest Bevin for the transport workers and Frank Hodge for the miners. Hodge was general secretary of the miners' union and during the negotiations he agreed to accept an offer whereby the government would maintain miners' wages at their old level, while negotiations went on with the mine-owners on other matters. The executive committee of the miners' union overruled their secretary and decided not to accept the offer. The railwaymen and transport workers used Hodge's acceptance as an excuse for calling off their threatened general strike a few hours before it was due to begin. 15 April, 1921, Black Friday, became a date of shame in trade union history. The miners went on with their strike until 1 July when they went back on worse terms than they could have had in April.

The defeat of the miners set the pattern for industry as a whole. Wages fell in every industry during 1921. With the failure of industrial action (or the strike) the workers turned again to political action and hoped that the return of a Labour government would lead to improvements. However the MacDonald government of 1924 with Philip Snowden as Chancellor of the Exchequer, soon showed that it had no new ideas for coping with unemployment and falling wages.

When the Labour government fell from power in 1924 Stanley Baldwin became Prime Minister with Winston Churchill as his Chancellor of the Exchequer. In 1925 he took Britain back on to the gold standard at pre-war rates. This meant

47 Winston Churchill leaving Number 11 Downing Street on his way to the Commons (April 1925). He was about to present his first budget which did nothing to help solve the economic problems of the country.

making the pound more expensive—it had cost only $4.02 up until 1925. After revaluation it would cost $4.86. This meant that all British exports cost more; thus if a load of coal worth £100 had cost $402 in 1924 now it would cost $486. This meant that it would be even harder to sell the now expensive British goods abroad.

The General Strike

The government and most economists and industrialists agreed that the cure

48 Herbert Smith arriving at Kingsway Hall, London, 14 May, 1926, for a meeting of the Miners' Federation. The miners were still on strike.

for this difficulty was a reduction in wages. Wage-cuts would lower prices, leading to increased sales of the cheaper goods. This in turn would lead to increased output, profits and employment. In particular this was the opinion of the mine-owners, who proposed that either the miners should work an eight-hour day (in place of the seven hours awarded them in 1919) or that they should accept wage-cuts.

The miners rejected this proposal, and the whole of the trade union movement rallied to their support. On Friday 31 July, 1925 Prime Minister Baldwin gave in before this united opposition. On this, Red Friday, he agreed to continue a government subsidy to mine owners so that they could maintain wages at their old rates while a Royal Commission examined the coal industry.

This was the sixth Royal Commission into the coal industry. The first, the

Sankey Commission in 1919, had, by a bare majority, advocated the nationalisation of the industry. The government had ignored this proposal, but had awarded the miners a seven-hour day and given the owners a subsidy which allowed them to continue to pay wages higher than they could otherwise have afforded.

This, the sixth Commission, headed by Sir Herbert Samuel, published its report in March 1926. It recommended that the industry should be reorganised; it suggested that the government should stop paying the subsidy and allow the industry to operate freely. It agreed that if the subsidy ended then either the miners would have to work a longer day, or wages would have to be cut.

This was what the owners had expected. It was also what the militant miners had feared. 'Not a penny off the pay, not a minute on the day' became the miners' slogan, coined by their syndicalist leader, A. J. Cook, and often voiced by their Yorkshire-born leader Herbert Smith. To offers of negotiation Smith's favourite reply was 'Nowt doing'.

The mine-owners' proposals, including the eight-hour day, were rejected on 30 April, 1926. The mine-owners then closed their pits; a lock-out was on. On 1 May the T.U.C. overwhelmingly agreed to call a general strike in support of the miners. The other unions remembered that the miners had been only the first to suffer wage reductions in 1921; they had all been affected later on. They feared that the same would happen in 1926, and their support for the miners was in part self-interested.

The general strike was fixed for 3 May; miners and other unions gave the General Council of the T.U.C. power to negotiate with the government and to settle the dispute.

Early on Sunday 2 May, the General Council agreed with a Cabinet committee to call off the strike while the subsidy continued and a solution was reached to the problems of the mines. The General Council went back to their headquarters only to find that the miners' leaders had left London on Saturday 1 May, to prepare for the strike. Throughout the whole of Sunday the Cabinet committee waited for an answer from the unions, while the General Council waited for the miners to return and agree to the terms of the settlement.

During this period of waiting a tired Cabinet encouraged by some extremists who wanted to fight with, and smash, the unions decided to take a harder line than they had agreed during their earlier negotiations. Late on Sunday evening Baldwin summoned the General Council to meet him. He said that printers at the *Daily Mail* had refused to print an editorial which condemned the threatened strike. This, said Baldwin, showed that negotiations were useless. The General Council was dismissed, Mr Baldwin went to bed and the General Strike was on.

As in 1921, the struggle was not between the mine-owners and workers. The whole union movement was now involved; so was the government. The unionists maintained that they wanted a settlement to an industrial problem—affecting the miners. The government, and in particular Winston Churchill, believed that

49 Armoured cars escorting lorries carrying food from London Docks to the food depot in Hyde Park (May 1926). This show of force annoyed the strikers who had not threatened violence, and believed it showed the government's intention to smash the workers' power.

the strike was an attempt by the workers to challenge the Parliamentary system of government. If the strike succeeded, they said, then the T.U.C. would be the real rulers of the country. This, of course, is what Owen had dreamed of, what the syndicalists worked for; it was not, however, what the leaders of the 1926 T.U.C. were striking for.

The strike was never really a general one. The T.U.C. only called out the miners, transport workers, railwaymen, dockers, printers, workers in power plants and in the steel, chemical and building trades. The response of these workers was almost unanimous.

Once the strike had started the leaders of the T.U.C. were faced with a number of problems. They had hoped that the mere threat of the strike would force the government to act. Once a few days had gone by, and the government had shown that they had prepared for the strike, the trade unionists could either have called the whole thing off, or they could have extended the strike, disrupting the country's economy even further. The moderate, legalistically-minded leaders were unwilling to follow this course; they were frightened of its consequences.

They were also alarmed at a speech made by Sir John Simon, a leading lawyer, who declared that the General Strike was illegal, and that all taking part in it were risking imprisonment. This was untrue, as we now know; the Trades Disputes Act 1927 was passed precisely to make such strikes illegal. The union leaders were less sure in 1926.

The government had prepared for the strike ever since Red Friday 1925; an Organisation for the Maintenance of Supplies had been set up to ensure that all essential supplies—food in particular—were distributed. The middle classes rallied to the support of the government, and the trains, buses, lorries ran, often with police support.

There were a number of examples of violence; buses were overturned, lorries stopped and burned; but in general it was a peaceful week. This horrified the Russians who had hoped to see the overthrow of the Parliamentary system and a violent uprising. Instead they saw the strikers at Plymouth playing a football game with the police.

The miners had given the leaders of the T.U.C. powers to negotiate. The moderate leaders, Arthur Pugh, J. H. Thomas and Ernest Bevin went to Mr Baldwin on 12 May to call off the strike. The miners alone refused to return; they stayed out until December when they were forced back, once again on worse terms than they were offered before the strike.

Consequences of the General Strike

The Conservative government then passed the Trades Disputes Act, 1927 which

50 Nottingham miners held a ballot in 1928 to decide whether they would join the company unions (which the owners favoured) or whether they would remain in the Nottingham Miners' Association. The ballot was conducted by the T.U.C. and showed a 9 to 1 majority in favour of staying in the old union.

made sympathetic (or general) strikes illegal. It also altered the law affecting the political levy. In future the unions could collect the levy only from those members who volunteered to pay it—or who 'contracted in'.

At first some employers tried to make the return to work difficult; some union members did not get their jobs back; other employers refused to allow unions to organise in their factories; some tried to form company unions.

Union leaders, and in particular Ernest Bevin of the Transport and General Workers Union and Walter Citrine, a leading member of the General Council of the T.U.C., decided that massive strikes such as that of 1926 were not worthwhile. Indeed contrary to popular myth British trade unions are nowadays reluctant to call a strike. The total number of working days lost per 1,000 workers in the leading industrial countries in 1963 was:

Italy	1,160
France	770
US	620
Norway	360
Canada	330
Australia	300
UK	140
Belgium	140
W. Germany	130
Sweden	10

51 Mr (now Lord) Citrine was a member of the T.U.C. General Strike Committee. Along with Ernest Bevin he worked hard to re-establish the influence of the trade-union movement after the collapse of 1926.

52 Transport House was opened by Ramsay MacDonald in 1928. It housed the national offices of the Transport and General Workers' Union, of the T.U.C. and of the Labour Party. To Bevin, the man most responsible for its building, it represented the trade union movement he was trying to create—responsible, organised and powerful.

This is, in large measure, the result of the influence of men such as Bevin. Addressing his union in 1945 he said:

> You are very proud of the accumulation of funds, but what has helped you to accumulate them? Arbitration for five years and no strikes. Although you may have £3,500,000 of money to date, if the tide turns and you have to pay strike pay . . . your surplus will vanish into thin air.

In general no union has sufficient funds to support a long strike; few unions have more than an average week's wage per member.

Bevin and other leaders realised that they could obtain their ends by negotiation and arbitration, at much less cost and with much less danger of rousing public hostility. Strikes are still called, of course, as the above figures show, and still more frequently strikes are threatened. Most strikes disrupt the economic life of the country, some affect our social life also. It is not surprising that the public at large dislike strikes, and allow their dislike of the weapon to spill over into hostility to the unions who use it. Mr Jack Scamp is the goverment-appointed 'trouble-shooter' one of whose tasks is to try and prevent industrial disputes reaching strike point. Another of his tasks is to investigate the causes of industrial unrest in the motor-vehicle industry. Almost invariably his reports on industrial disputes show that when an industrial dispute develops to the point where a strike breaks out management has failed in communicating with the workers.

Even in 1926 some employers, among them Sir Alfred Mond of Imperial Chemical Industries, recognised that organised trade unionism was an important feature of British industrial life. In 1928 he led a group of industrialists in talks with union representatives headed by Ben Turner, then chairman of the T.U.C. These Mond-Turner talks were a sign that employers and unions were prepared to work together. The one side would give up the dream of the syndicalists, the other would give up the nineteenth-century attitudes of opposition to unionism.

Not all workers were convinced of the value of such 'collaboration with the enemy'. Not all employers accepted that improved labour-management relations were of great value. However during the war, 1939–45, joint consultative committees were set up to lessen the danger of friction between employers and their workers, and to try and raise the production and productivity of each factory. These committees functioned at national level, where union leaders negotiated with employers' leaders, and at shop floor level, where the local union representatives or men elected from the shop floor negotiated with the local manager.

Since 1945 this dialogue between labour and management has increased as more industries and firms have adopted the idea of improving labour relations. This has led to a lessening of the class conflict between labour and capital. British

53 Sir Alfred Mond, MP for Swansea and Chairman of Imperial Chemical Industries, in 1922.

54 Ben Turner (formerly chairman of the T.U.C.) was Minister for Mines in the Labour Government of 1929. Here he is going to a Cabinet meeting.

trade unions still lag behind their American counterparts whose leaders actively encourage management to introduce labour-saving machinery. American unions have even bought firms which were unwilling to modernise quickly enough. British trade unions have not gone this far, but they have willingly accepted the introduction of machinery, and at factory level have helped to increase total production as well as the productivity of the individual worker.

Indeed, Britain's remarkable post-war recovery could not have taken place without this attitude on the part of the workers and management. The A.E.U. is proud to point out that productivity per man in engineering, shipbuilding and electrical goods, in 1950, was well over 40% higher than in 1946, and in the vehicles section of the industry between 60 and 70% higher.

Further Reading
Lord Citrine: *Men at Work* (Hutchinson)
J. Symons: *The General Strike* (Cresset)
F. Williams: *A Pattern of Rulers* (Longmans)

7 From the General Strike to 1945

The Depression

The 1930s are infamous as the years of economic depression. Three million workers were unemployed between 1931 and 1933, and after a fall to one and a half million, the level of unemployment had begun to rise again until in 1938 the rearmament programme created more work in Britain's heavy industries. The trade union movement supported ideas put forward by J. M. Keynes, who

55 J. M. Keynes whose ideas for solving our economic problems were rejected by orthodox financiers and politicians such as Winston Churchill and Philip Snowden.

56 Upholstering and trimming the bodies of cars on an assembly line at Morris Motors, Cowley, Oxford, in 1930. There were cleaner surroundings and lighter work for those who escaped the Depression.

favoured a vast increase in state activity and spending as a cure for unemployment. One aspect of state activity which the movement supported was nationalisation, or state ownership of industry. T.U.C. reports in favour of the nationalisation of steel (1934), cotton (1935), coal and electricity (1936), contained recommendations as to the method of state control. These reports were useful to the Labour government which came to power in 1945 with a programme of nationalising some industries.

The older industries, such as cotton, coal, shipbuilding and iron and steel, were those in which unemployment levels were the highest. Strikes were frequent in these industries as the unions tried to stop employers lowering wages.

During these years of depression there was a continual growth in new industries, such as the chemical, motor-vehicle and electrical engineering industries. There was also an increase in the numbers employed in service industries, such as insurance, distribution and entertainment. In these industries unions struggled for recognition. In 1932 over 8,000 workers at the Austin car plant went on strike for better wages and permission to allow unions to organise the workers in the factory; in 1935 workers at the Hawker Aircraft factories organised a strike to gain union recognition. Their success encouraged workers in other factories.

The new industries employed a different kind of craftsman from those working in the older, heavier industries. This meant that new unions had to be formed (e.g. the Electrical Trades Union), some of the old unions grew rapidly (e.g. the Amalgamated Engineering Union) while some of the once strong unions became less powerful (e.g. the unions organising workers in the textile industries). A large proportion of the workers in the new industries were unskilled or semi-skilled; they did not need to have served an apprenticeship or learned a craft. Many of these workers joined one of the General Unions, which led to the growth of the National Union of General and Municipal Workers, and of the Transport and General Workers Union which in 1937, with a membership of over 650,000, became the largest union in the world.

57 A union-management meeting at the Ford works, Dagenham. 40,000 Ford workers are represented by 39 unions.

58 The A.E.U. provided £4,000 for medical supplies for Spanish refugees in France, 1939. Fascists demonstrated against this support for left-wing aliens.

The syndicalists had hoped that industrial unions (one union for each industry) might develop in Britain. Such hopes were not shared by the leaders of the existing unions who supported a T.U.C. report on Union Structure (1927) which argued in favour of the union system which had developed over the past 70 years or so. This view was also expressed in similar T.U.C. reports in 1944 and 1962. So whereas there is one union to speak for car workers at Ford's Detroit Works, British workers at Ford's, Dagenham, are represented by 39 different unions. This makes union-management negotiation complicated, and also allows for a good deal of inter-union rivalry and demarcation disputes as various unions claim the right to do a certain job.

A rise in the standard of living of many workers in Mid-Victorian Britain was noted in Chapter 3. This improvement in general living standards continued during the first half of this century, even during the depressed years of the 1930s.

The cost of imports into Britain—of food and raw material—fell drastically during the late 1920s and early 1930s. In part this was one cause of the world's depression; the primary countries received less for their produce and so were able to buy less from the manufacturing countries. On the other hand, the fall

59 Ernest Bevin in 1940. The forceful leader of the transport workers was to be a tireless Minister.

in import prices meant that the cost of living fell, and as most incomes remained fairly stable, life was better in the 1930s than in the 1920s for all classes—unskilled, skilled, unemployed and disabled.

Indices of Income in the United Kingdom at 1900 prices (1900 = 100)

Year	Index of National Income	Index of Income per head
1913	120.3	108.4
1923–24	115.3	106.0
1929	132	118.8
1931–32	129.3	115.2
1937	155.4	135.1

The 1930s and the depression created conditions favourable to the growth of dictatorships in Europe. Hitler in Germany, Mussolini in Italy, Franco in Spain, Stalin in Russia, were the most prominent of the dictators. The trade union movement was violently opposed to the Russian Communist system; it was equally opposed to Fascism and Nazism. This opposition led the unions to support the Republican Government in Spain when it was attacked by General Franco backed by Italy and Germany. The continued aggression of Germany caused the T.U.C. to call for a programme of rearmament (1934). This was exactly one hundred years since the Tolpuddle Martyrs had been condemned. At one celebration to mark this centenary, Ernest Bevin, leader of the Transport and General Workers Union, declared, 'Whenever I am asked about the dictatorship of the proletariat, of the Nazis or any other form of it, I reply that I was born in a village and held under it until I was fourteen—and I will see you to the devil before I have any more.'

The Trade Unions During the War

The Chamberlain Government which declared war on Germany in 1939 almost ignored the contribution the trade union movement and individual unions might make towards the war effort. When Winston Churchill became Prime Minister in 1940, there was an abrupt change in attitudes. He immediately invited Ernest Bevin, not then even a Member of Parliament, to become Minister of Labour. His Ministry persuaded the unions to accept direction of labour. Some industries and trades were classified as 'essential'; no worker was allowed to leave an essential occupation, employers in such industries could recruit extra labour only through the local offices of the Ministry of Labour.

60 Sir (later Lord) William Beveridge at an interview in March 1942. This was the Beveridge year when he presented his report and spoke at hundreds of meetings throughout the country.

61 Low, the cartoonist, always portrayed the trade-union movement as a carthorse—strong, slow, harmless and a little stupid. This cartoon shows the T.U.C. freeing itself from restrictions (which will upset the socialist apple-cart) so that it can follow the lambs, 'no wages policy' and 'no direction'.

As in the First World War so in the Second. Unions gave up many of their hard won privileges; they allowed 'dilution' of labour which led to an increased production of war material. Union members were active in arbitration councils set up to solve industrial disputes, and in countless advisory councils and productivity boards.

Quite early in the war the Churchill government set up various bodies to lay plans for post-war Britain. The trade union movement was active in preparing evidence for these bodies. In 1942, together with the National Union of Teachers, the Workers' Educational Association and the Co-operative Unions, the T.U.C. produced a Report on Education which called for the reforms later to be included in the 1944 Education Act. In 1942 Sir William Beveridge produced his famous

Report which called for a huge increase in public spending as the means of attacking the five giant evils—Want, Disease, Ignorance, Squalor and Idleness. While the Coalition government showed a lukewarm attitude towards the Report, and Labour Ministers in this Government, particularly Herbert Morrison, argued that it was too idealistic, the T.U.C. supported a plan which, if implemented, would create a new society. Sir William Beveridge acknowledged his debt to the union movement when he called the unions 'the Godfathers of the Beveridge Report'.

This Report and a government White Paper on Full Employment (1944) caused the T.U.C. to set out its own ideas in an *Interim Report on Post War Reconstruction* (1944). This examined the meaning and implications of full employment. The T.U.C. hoped that post-war governments would use the state's powers to ensure that there would be no depression as there had been in 1921. By this time, the ideas put forward by J. M. Keynes had become accepted by most economists and politicians. Beveridge and the T.U.C. used his ideas in developing their own policies for full employment.

Beveridge and the T.U.C. recognised that one problem resulting from full employment would be wage-inflation. Almost everyone would have a job. If an employer wanted to recruit extra labour he would have to offer higher wages to attract men from their existing place of work. Their current employer would not want to lose his workers, so he would counter this offer by an even higher offer. In this situation trade unions could use the scarcity of labour as a strong bargaining counter in their negotiations with employers, and wage rates could again be driven up.

The T.U.C. Report (1944) promised that if governments used their powers to guarantee full employment, and took steps to stop prices and profits from rising, the T.U.C. would not use its powers to drive up wages. This was the first of many statements on 'a wages policy'. The unions refused to give up their right to bargain with employers on behalf of their members; they refused to accept the need for government interference in wage-negotiations. On the other hand, they promised that they would voluntarily curb their demands, provided that prices and profits were limited.

Further Reading
C. L. Mowat, *Britain between the Wars, 1918–1940* (Methuen)
S. Pollard: *Development of the British Economy, 1914–1950* (Arnold)
B. Wootton: *Social Foundations of Wages Policy* (Allen & Unwin)

8 Unions in the Post-War World

Full Employment and the Welfare State

In 1945 the Labour Party won the election.

This was the trade unions' own party from which the unions expected a number of reforms and for which they were prepared to honour the spirit of their 1944 Report on wages and productivity. Led by Mr Attlee, Herbert Morrison and Ernest Bevin this government proceeded to pass Acts of Parliament to implement the recommendations of the many Reports, such as Beveridge's. The trade unions had had many years of experience as friendly societies, and the Labour government took advantage of this experience and recruited trade union personnel into the various Ministries responsible for the working of the National Insurance

62 Labour leaders, Bevin, Attlee and Morrison, with their supporters at the Victory Hall, Leicester Square, on election night, August 1945.

63 A youthful-looking Harold Wilson and a sick Stafford Cripps leaving Number 10 Downing Street in 1950.

Acts, the National Health Service Act, the National Assistance Board Act, etc.

For many reasons the demand for labour remained high after 1945. One of the main causes was the need for a vast increase in British exports. Before the War a large part of Britain's imports was paid for by interest on British investments in overseas countries. During the War over £3,000 million of these investments had to be sold to pay for imports, so after the War more of our imports had to be paid for by exports; it was also expected that the volume of imports would rise above the 1939 level after 1945 as imported machinery and material was brought in to help reconstruct war-damaged Britain.

Full employment was at last a reality. The trade unions, as they had promised in the 1944 Report, did not abuse their powers. In 1948 Sir Stafford Cripps, Chancellor of the Exchequer, proposed a period of wage-freeze during which the unions would not ask for any wage increases. This, it was hoped, would allow the prices of British exports to remain stable so that more could be sold. This freeze was maintained throughout 1948 and 1949. Unfortunately, the prices of many imports, such as food and raw materials, rose as the world demand for these goods was higher than world supply. Stable wage rates and rising prices meant that the workers' standard of living fell. The T.U.C. therefore called off the wage freeze in 1950.

Changing Political Attitudes

In 1951 a Conservative government came to power. A minority of unionists wanted to use the power of the trade union movement as a weapon against this government.

But trade union leaders had now become less politically conscious. They had seen that nationalisation was not the cure-all for the workers' problems; industrial relations in the nationalised coal industry were less rancorous than they had been in the 1920s, but strikes were frequent and bitter; the workers on British Railways had as little say in management decisions as they had had in the days of private enterprise. Meanwhile, full employment and the social security of the welfare state provided the working man with an even higher standard of living. In the opinion of many union members there seemed little that political activity could do for him, especially since the new Conservative government promised to continue the employment and welfare policies of its Labour predecessor.

So, while trade unions continued to affiliate to the Labour Party, an increasing number of union members refused to pay the political levy, while more and more voted Conservative at the General Elections in the 1950s. The T.U.C. itself declared in 1951:

64 Sir (later Lord) Walter Monckton was Minister of Labour in the Churchill government in 1951. He was an advocate of negotiation and a symbol to the unions of the changes that had taken place in the Conservative Party.

> Since the Conservative administration of pre-war days, the range of consultation between Ministers and both sides of industry has considerably increased, and the machinery of joint consultation has enormously improved. We expect of this government that they will maintain to the full this practice of consultation. On our part, we shall continue to examine every question solely in the light of its industrial and economic implications.

A T.U.C. report, 1952, declared:

> At the same time, with industry playing such an important part in the economic position of the country and in the determination of the standard of living of our people, the General Council and the trade union Movement resolutely turned down suggestions that political opposition to the government and its policy should be reinforced by industrial action.

The union movement did not imitate the American unions which have never formed a political party nor given unswerving loyalty to either of the two major parties. The British trade union movement had been involved with the development of the Labour Party from its beginning; this involvement is too deep and has too many memories for it to be lightly broken. Ted Hill was the General Secretary of the Boilermakers when in 1963 he said, 'I don't trust the Tories; I would not trust them further than I can throw them—and I'm an old man.' This apparently immovable hostility to the 'other party' ensures the continuance of the support of most union members and nearly all union leaders for the Labour Party.

The Conservative government, 1951–64, was very different from the Conservative governments of pre-war days. When one of its leading members, R. A. Butler, was asked to comment on the need for a little unemployment as a solution to wage-inflation, he said: 'People who talk of a pool of unemployment ought to be thrown into it'. Walter Monkton, Minister of Labour in the Churchill government, set the pattern for Conservative attitudes to labour relations. He used the power of the Ministry to try to settle industrial disputes without strikes.

The Conservative government was also different to its Labour predecessors. It coined the slogan 'Set the people free'. This freedom meant the end of economic planning; it meant that the state would not set limits to profit levels, nor would it hold down prices. As Frank Cousins pointed out this meant that the unions were also free to get the best possible bargain they could for their members.

Public Hostility to the Unions

By this time the unions had learned to use their strength to negotiate at least annual wages increases. Many workers had ceased to think of a wage as a return for work and effort and had come to think of it as an income to maintain their family at a certain standard of living. If the cost of living rose, then, many workers assumed, wages should rise to ensure that their living standards were maintained. It was during this period that post-war public hostility to the unions became most noticeable. The workers increased their share of the national output as employers granted wage increases and passed the extra cost along to the consumer in the shape of higher prices.

For many workers the standard of living rose so remarkably that Mr Macmillan could declare in 1957: 'They have never had it so good.' For a minority, however, inflation meant a fall in living standards. Workers with weak unions, professional people often with no union at all, people living on fixed incomes or retirement pensions suffered as prices continued to rise. There were still others whose standard of living rose less quickly than did that of the newly emancipated workers.

This caused a good deal of resentment and led to complaints that unions were abusing their power. Paradoxically, the loudest and most frequent complaints were made by economists and politicians who advocated an end to government

65 Harold Macmillan speaking at the Tory Party Conference, 13 October, 1958. Whether or not he was responsible for the prosperity of the late 1950s, he and the Tory Party were helped into office on the strength of this affluence.

66 The affluence of the late 1950s created a number of economic problems. Vicky shows Selwyn Lloyd (Chancellor of the Exchequer) leaving 'freedom' behind as he tries to hitch a ride from Harold Wilson (Leader of the Opposition) towards a planned economy.

regulation and a dismantling of the structure of the welfare state—in the name of freedom. These critics would have curbs put on the freedom of unions to use their power while allowing complete freedom to industry and commerce to maximise their profits. This, as union leaders have pointed out, is unrealistic; 'if freedom works then it works for everyone' said one union leader.

With a rise in living standards the volume of imports of more and different foods and more raw materials to make the goods demanded by the increasingly affluent working class rose. Meanwhile, exports did not rise as quickly; since manufacturers could sell their goods at home there was no need for them to engage in the difficult task of selling them abroad. This was the cause of the frequent balance of payments crises which ultimately led a Conservative Chancellor of the Exchequer, Selwyn Lloyd, to reject the policy of freedom in favour of economic planning.

Further Reading
S. Pollard: *The Development of the British Economy, 1914–1950* (Arnold)
C. D. N. Worswick and P. H. Ady: *The British Economy, 1945–50* (O.U.P.)
A. Shonfield: *British Economic Policy since the War* (Penguin)

9 Unions and Modern Economic Planning

It is possible that future historians will see 1961 as a decisive year in British economic development. In that year Britain first applied to join the European Economic Community, or Common Market, a step which she had refused to take in the headier days of the 1950s. In that year also the Conservative government, which had preached the virtues of freedom in the 1950s, decided to set up the National Economic Development Council, to plan the future development of the British economy. Most significant for the trade unions was the setting up of the National Incomes Commission which the government hoped to use to regulate the pattern of wage demands and increases. These new bodies were soon christened Neddy and Nicky.

67 In June 1961 Vicky portrayed Macmillan having a nightmare in which he sees President Kennedy officiating at the marriage of Britain to a booming Miss Europe. The wedding has still to take place.

68 The first meeting of the N.E.D.C., March 1962. Trade union leaders occupy most of the chairs of the right of the picture.

Neddy was called to its first meeting in March 1962. Here representatives of the government, industry and the union movement met to work out plans for future economic development. In 1963 little Neddies (or Economic Development Committees) were set up to examine economic performance in various sectors of British industry, and to suggest how each industry would be affected by the over-all plans being worked out by Neddy. On all these Committees and Councils trade union representatives were active, a sign that unions accepted the responsibility of their new power, that the government recognised the reality of this power and that industrialist and government accepted the unions as equal partners.

Nicky had a less happy beginning. In July 1961 Mr Selwyn Lloyd imposed a pay pause, announcing that for an indefinite time the government would not allow any wage or salary increases. This singled out wages and salaries as the causes of inflation, an opinion not universally held; it ignored, for instance, the possibilities of rises in profits and prices, which the T.U.C. Report, 1944, considered to be of equal importance with wage rates.

If the late 1950s were years in which the population at large 'had never had it so good', they were also years in which shareholders enjoyed great increases in the value of their shares. Newspaper reports familiarised people with the stock exchange boom; advertisements by unit trust groups pointed out that if one invested £100 on 1 January, 1951 it would have been worth over £700 by 1 January, 1967. As can be seen from the following table much wealth is created for those fortunate enough to have investments:

Ordinary Share Index
(1st July 1935 = 100)
End of January 1958 = 163·2
1959 = 212·8
1960 = 329·6

Vicky
AFTER THE FAMOUS
RECRUITING POSTER

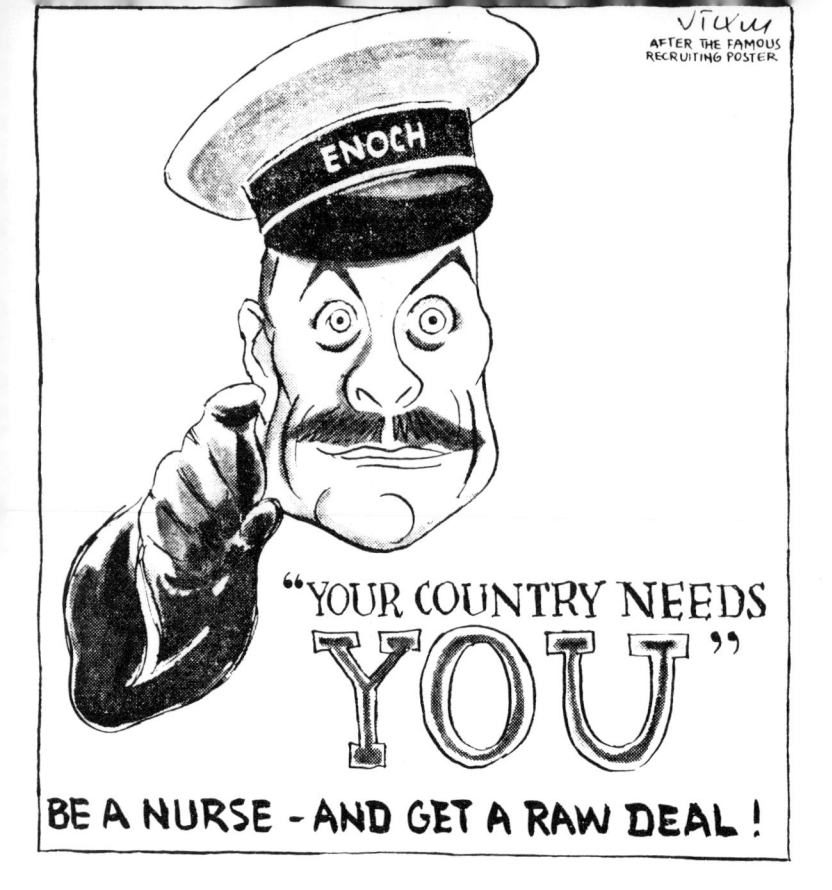

"YOUR COUNTRY NEEDS YOU"

BE A NURSE - AND GET A RAW DEAL!

69 This Vicky cartoon shows the Minister of Health (Enoch Powell) appealing for more people to become poorly-paid nurses. Immigrant nurses have saved the hospital service from collapse.

Employees in the public service suffered most during this period, as their employer, the government, could ensure that the pay pause was observed in their case. Others suffered in inverse ratio to the strength of their union; the electricians challenged the government when the union had been awarded a pay increase which the Central Electricity Board, under the direction of the Minister of Fuel and Power, threatened not to honour. The union went ahead with plans for a strike of electricians in the power industry. At the last minute the Minister intervened, agreed to pay the increased wage and the strike was called off. Nurses, having only a weak union, and being unwilling to use the threat of a strike, were less fortunate.

With the coming to power of the Labour Government in 1964, the Department of Economic Affairs was set up to co-ordinate economic planning. The T.U.C. and individual unions were invited to work with the new Department to prepare facts and figures on which Britain's first ever Economic Plan was to be based. This Plan, published in 1965, had in one sense a limited value. Within months of its publication the Labour government applied a series of massive deflationary measures (July 1966) which rendered the Plan's assumptions null and void. In another sense, however, this failure made the trade union movement more determined to make economic planning work. The T.U.C. Report to Neddy (1967) and its first ever Annual Economic Review (1968) called for increased government intervention at industry and firm level, to bring about the changes required to ensure a higher level of economic growth. The setting up of the Industrial Reorganisation Committee was one response of the government to these T.U.C. demands.

In December 1964 Mr George Brown, Minister in charge of the Department of Economic Affairs, announced the signing of a Declaration of Intent. The government, industry and the T.U.C. had agreed to co-operate in tackling the problems of productivity, prices and incomes. The National Board for Prices and Incomes, a successor to Nicky, was set up. The triple partners in the signing of the Intent agreed that in future wage increases would normally only be awarded when increased output per man (or increased productivity) warranted it. However, a high demand for labour, the result of the maintenance of full employment, and the continuation of individual trade union bargaining with employers meant that, in spite of the Intent, wages still rose more quickly than output.

The General Council of the T.U.C. had already been given increased powers by individual unions. They had agreed, for example, not to call a strike until they had notified the General Council of the T.U.C. This Council would then use its influence to try and settle the dispute, so that members of other unions would not be thrown out of work by a strike. In 1965 the various unions gave the General Council some say in wage bargaining. In future each union would notify the General Council when it decided to apply for a wage increase; the General Council hoped that it might have the time to examine these claims, see whether the demand was justified and, possibly, persuade the union concerned to modify

70 The Minister for Economic Affairs, George Brown, with representatives of industry (on his right) and the T.U.C. at the signing of the Declaration of Intent, December 1964.

or withdraw the demand if the General Council considered there was no justification for a wage increase.

In 1966 the T.U.C. supported the government's call for a wage freeze. At the same time it expressed anxiety about the government's intention to introduce legislation which would give them the power to interfere in the process of wage bargaining. The unions were against such interference, even if it came from a union-supported Labour government. The T.U.C. proposed that the unions should run their own vetting system; this scheme was approved by the unions. By now, however, the government had strengthened the powers of the Prices and Incomes Board. Unions and employers had now to submit schemes for wage demands and possible increases to the Board, which had the power to accept, amend or reject the suggestions. Unions or employers who then ignored the findings of the Board risked imprisonment. In one sense this was a return to the Parliament-magistrate wage regulation of pre-industrial Britain.

Redundancy

Trade union leaders had for a long time realised that living standards depended

71 George Woodcock signing the joint agreement on productivity (July 1967). With him are John Davies of C.B.I., Sir Harry Douglass of the T.U.C. and Sir Stephen Brown of C.B.I.

72 Ray Gunter, Minister of Labour, at the opening of the Poplar Government Training Centre, April 1968. Another skilled workman is being trained.

on increasing productivity. This was why they agreed with the C.B.I. to sign a joint declaration on productivity (July 1967). Increasing productivity often means that one man and a machine do the work formerly done by two or more men and a less efficient machine. This process requires the training of the one workman so that he can use the machine. It also requires the re-training of the now unwanted workers so that they can be employed at some new task. Trade unions were willing partners with industry and the government in the setting up of re-training centres.

Redundancy was one of the many 'new' words which became popular in the 1960s; in former years people had spoken of unemployment. There is of course a real difference between unemployment, as it was understood in pre-war Britain, and redundancy from which an increasing number of workers were to suffer in the 1960s. There does exist some hope of a man getting some job in a time of full employment. There was little or no hope of getting a job in pre-war depressed areas.

However, redundant workers pose at least two problems. First there is the problem of re-training. Then there is a period of time during which the displaced worker has to look for a new job. Some industries, notably the nationalised coal and railway industries, had worked out redundancy payment schemes. Under these a redundant workman received a lump sum, tax-free payment from his former employer, as a sort of cushion against unemployment. The Labour government passed a Redundancy Payments Act which made such payments compulsory for all industries and firms when they dismiss a workman. The government also improved the unemployment benefits payments system; in future benefits would be related to a man's earnings, so that a man who had enjoyed £20 a week and a certain standard of living would not be reduced to a subsistence pittance when he was made redundant. This also helped to soften the blow of losing his job and it was hoped would persuade more workers to accept technological change and redundancy more easily than they would have done if redundancy had meant great economic hardship.

White-Collar Unions

Redundancy and productivity were the consequences of the technological revolution which is the modern continuation of the 'industrial revolution'. In the technological revolution machinery, automated plant and computer systems replace manpower. A different type of workman was required to build and maintain this complicated technological equipment. To organise the new labour force, new unions came into being or were enlarged. The Association of Scientific, Technical and Managerial Staff, and the Draughtsmen's and Allied Technician's Association recruit the highly-paid, highly-qualified and scarce white-collar workers. These men had no bitter memories of the 1930s; they welcomed talk of increasing productivity; their members would be building and maintaining the new machinery.

These were not the first white-collar unions as was seen in Chapter 4. In post-war Britain there was an increase in the membership of many of these older unions and a growth in the number of such unions. There was also increasing militancy on the part of these 'respectable' workers. More of these white-collar unions affiliated to the T.U.C., as did the National Association of Local Government Officers (N.A.L.G.O.) whose members include Town Clerks and City Librarians.

Why did more teachers, nurses and bank clerks join trade unions? Salaried people had, by and large, done less well than the 'workers' during the wage-

"THAT'S THE REASON THEY'RE CALLED LESSONS," THE GRYPHON REMARKED: "BECAUSE THEY LESSEN FROM DAY TO DAY."
— ALICE IN WONDERLAND

73 In May 1961 teachers threatened to go on strike. The middle classes were learning that 'might' was accepted as 'right'.

chasing-prices spiral of the 1950s. An increasing number of salaried people believed that union activity was one cause of the improved status of the wage-earner. They hoped, perhaps, that similar activity on their part might lead to similar improvement in their status. These salaried unions were soon involved in traditional trade union activity; teachers went on strike, bank clerks picketed strike-bound banks, go-slow and work-to-rule campaigns were organised by teachers. To date these campaigns seem to have succeeded; bank clerks have been awarded two large pay increases and look like succeeding in ending Saturday work in the banks; teachers no longer have to supervise school meals — the purpose of their most recent campaign.

Future Trends

The history of the trade union movement has been one of continuous development. There is no reason to suppose that its future will be any different. It seems likely, for example, that the powers of the General Council, or some such similar body, will continue to grow. The General Council was set up in 1921, to help individual unions to organise, to assist unions in preparing schemes for union amalgamation. By 1968, as we have seen, it had been granted the right to be notified when unions intended to call a strike, and it had persuaded unions to accept central guidance on wage claims. The General Strike indicated that one of the weaknesses of the union movement was the absence of some central body, with adequate powers, to which all unions would cede some of their powers and rights. While the tradition of individual union activity remains strong, there is some evidence that the General Council is being allowed to take over some of the unions' traditional roles. This is a trend which might well continue to develop.

The amalgamation of trade unions began over a century ago. The local unions which started the movement have now disappeared. The trend of fewer, larger unions continues today. Indeed, it is almost inevitable if the workers are to be adequately represented in negotiations with employers, who are amalgamating into fewer, larger firms. Each day we read of one or more take-overs in industry; for various economic reasons it is likely that this process will continue.

If unions do grow larger there is a danger that their leaders will be out of touch with their followers. This fear is one which is shared by many unionists. They recall the careers of pre-war leaders; John Hodge, for example, entitled his autobiography: *From Workman's Cottage to Windsor Castle*; J. H. Thomas, the N.U.R. leader, was well known for his admiration for the upper classes and willingly followed Ramsay MacDonald's lead in what is known as the great betrayal of 1931.

Communication between leaders and members could be maintained if there were more full-time officials. This, however, would mean that union members would have to pay higher union fees than they do at present. Members hate to increase their subscriptions which, for the A.E.U., were 4% of wages in 1912, but only 1% in 1959, and which on average for all trade unions were ·75% of basic wages in 1958 compared to 1·5% in 1939.

The legal position of trade unions is again uncertain. One hundred years ago the Sheffield outrages led to the appointment of one Royal Commission which was followed by the passing of three major Acts affecting trade unions. When a former shop steward of D.A.T.A. left the union, it threatened to call a strike if his employers at London Airport continued to employ the non-unionist. The employers gave in to this threat and dismissed him. He prosecuted his former union and in 1964 the House of Lords decided that whereas unions had the power to strike, paradoxically they had no right to threaten to do so. A number of court

74 Bank clerks picketing a bank in Cardiff, November 1967, during their first-ever strike. This strike was successful and the employers were forced to recognise the National Union of Bank Employees' right to negotiate the wages of their members. Previously only company unions (or staff associations) were recognised.

cases after this and their decisions showed that the legal position of unions was uncertain.

This uncertainty was resolved in 1964 when the Labour government passed a Trades Disputes Act which affirmed each union's right to use the strike and to threaten to do so. This Act was followed by the setting up of a Royal Commission on Trade Unions and Employers Associations. This, the Donovan Commission, has just issued its Report. It is highly likely that, as happened one hundred years ago, legislation will follow the publication of this Report.

Further Reading
A. Sampson: *Macmillan: A Study in Ambiguity* (Penguin)
R. Bevins: *The Greasy Pole* (Hodder)
M. Stewart: *Frank Cousins* (Hutchinson)

10 Organisation

Like Topsy the trade union movement 'just growed'; there was no blue-print or plan, no other country's experience which could be used as a model to construct a British trade union movement. The growth of different unions at different rates and in different industrial circumstances has led to a great variety in union structure and organisation.

75 Trade union executives at Central Hall, Westminster, listen to George Woodcock, General Secretary of the

Unions at the Local Level

At the basis of all unions is the branch, the local unit which the new member joins. A branch may consist of workers from a number of other factories, shops or offices or it may consist of workers from only one factory or workshop. The branch officials—chairman, treasurer and secretary—are members who carry out their union duties in addition to doing a normal day's work, and usually they are elected by branch members. The attendance at branch meetings is rarely very large and few people are anxious to allow their names to go forward for the time-consuming and unrewarding jobs of branch officers. This has given an opportunity to dedicated people among whom have been communist members of unions.

T.U.C., proposing a T.U.C. incomes policy. This proposal was accepted and strengthened the power of the T.U.C.

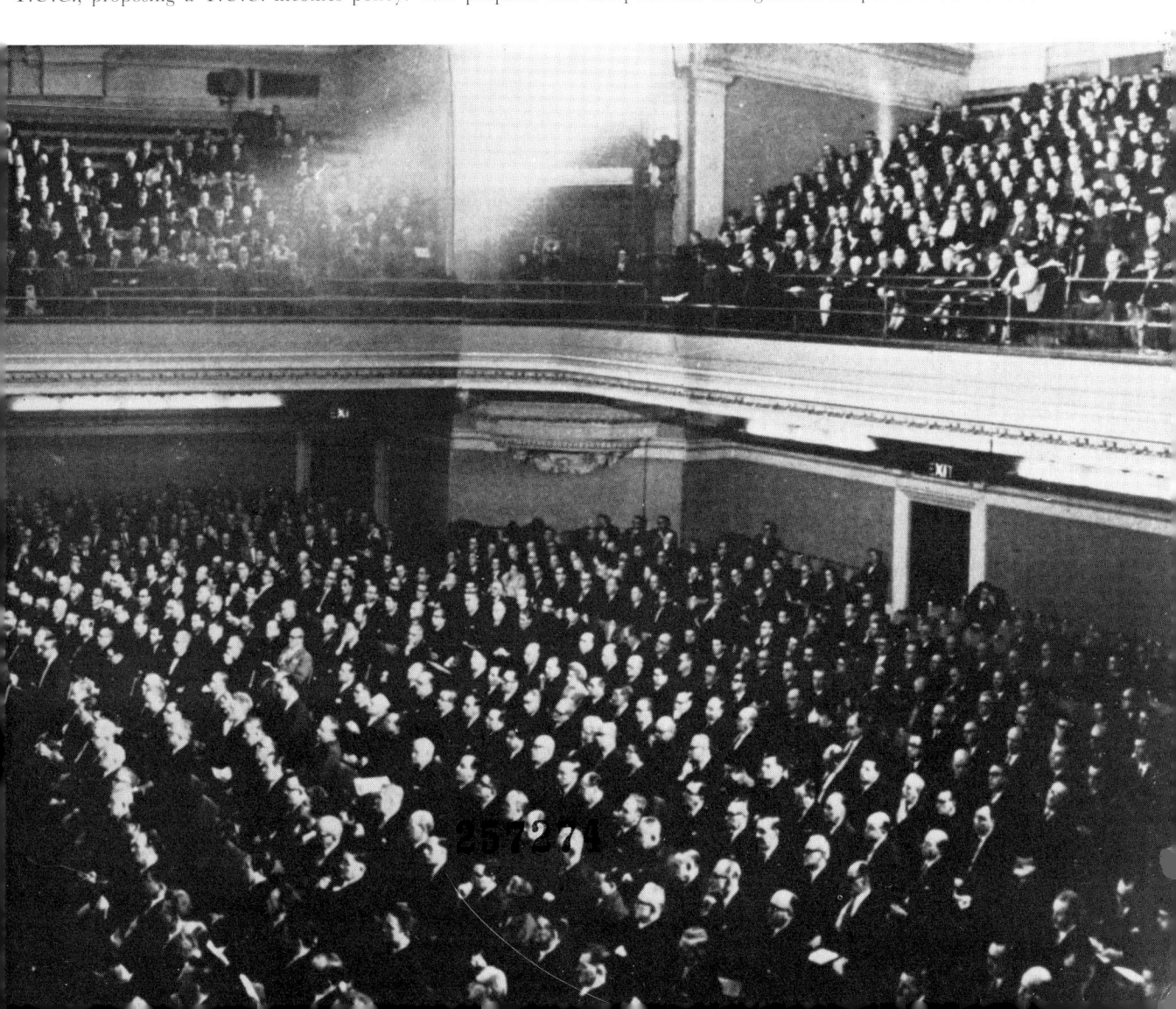

The shop steward is the man who at the shop-floor level collects the union subscriptions, recruits new members, and is the workers' representative on factory committees. He makes sure that management honours national agreements and frequently he negotiates local agreements with management without recourse to the union's head office. In many cases these local agreements supersede the national agreement and emphasise in the mind of the worker the importance of the shop steward. He gains in popularity as the full-time officers seem remote, dilatory and relatively less successful in advancing the workers' cause.

Membership of a union is compulsory in industries in which the unions have won the 'closed-shop' principle. In such industries no one may be employed unless he is a member of a particular union. The miners and other union members which have established this principle argue that since it is the union which has won the improved pay and conditions which apply in an industry, it is therefore only fair that those who enjoy these benefits should subscribe to the funds which pay the negotiators and officials. This argument is one of the main causes of public hostility to trade unionism in the post-war period. It suggests compulsion and dictatorship which offends the traditional liberalism of British life.

A number of branches will be joined to form a district which, in turn, will be grouped with others to form regions or areas. Each of these may cover a wide geographical area where the branches are few and scattered; there may, however, be several districts in a relatively small but highly industrialised and densely populated area. The officials who run these sections of the union are usually full-time officers paid by their union. In some unions they are elected by members, in others, as in the Transport and General Workers Union, all full-time officers are appointed by the national executive.

The Central Organisation

The national executive committee of a union may have a great deal of power (as in the case of the N.U.R.), or it may be constitutionally under the guidance of a more powerfully established general secretary (as happens in the Transport and General Workers Union). The national executive may be a policy-making body which has only to report to a biennial and relatively impotent conference of union delegates, or it may be merely a body for carrying out the policy defined by a conference. Most unions hold an annual conference of delegates (representing their different districts) where resolutions on a wide variety of industrial, economic, social and political matters will be considered.

In the public mind the union is best represented by its general secretary. Some of these are more important than others; when Ernest Bevin was working out the organisation of his union (T.G.W.U.) in the early 1920s he made sure that the

76 Present and future leaders of the trade-union movement attend the T.U.C. Training College. Here the T.U.C.'s medical adviser takes a class on health in industry.

most important and powerful person in the union was the general secretary, the only officer in the union elected by a national ballot of all union members. Other general secretaries are apparently less powerful. Thus Sidney Greene of the N.U.R. always makes it clear that he is 'referring the matter back to my executive', while William Carron of the A.E.U. often found his decisions reversed by the executive.

Some general secretaries such as Ted Hill, are militants of the old school; a larger number are men such as Harry Douglass, secretary of the Iron and Steel Trades Confederation. He is a business-minded leader. As he said at the 1961 T.U.C. meeting: 'The trade union movement today is a very powerful machine, and it can only be driven by experts'.

The T.U.C.

Most unions are members of the T.U.C., although some white-collar unions remain outside the Congress as they are suspicious of its political connections. The T.U.C. has an elected General Council of 34 of the general secretaries of member unions which meets once a month at Congress House in Bloomsbury. The T.U.C. has very little power over member unions, which it can only advise or try to persuade but cannot command. Its weakness is reflected in its financial state. The unions pay only 1s. per year per member to the T.U.C., giving it an annual income of about £500,000 from which it has to pay staff, provide scholarships, publicity, international affiliation fees and the organising of the annual conference.

Having little power and money the T.U.C. has also too small a staff. Only 96 people are employed at Congress House to research into matters concerning the union movement which they also help to direct. Increasingly the T.U.C. has been involved in the economic life of the country and its Economic Committee under the chairmanship of Harry Douglass is an active partner in N.E.D.C. As he said at the 1963 Congress:

> Trade unions have for too long been kept on the defensive. We must seize the initiative wherever we can. We have a right and a duty to help shape planning and we must recognise that the nature and methods of trade unions will be shaped by it ... If we are afraid of planning, afraid that it will challenge our own forms of conservatism, then let us say so here and now and have done with it. But if we do accept it ... to open a way to a better future for the working people of Britain and other countries—then we must be prepared to justify our attitudes, our practices, and indeed the structure of our organisations.

Possibly the best known member of the union movement is George Woodcock, general secretary of the T.U.C. He worked as a half-timer at the age of twelve in a cotton mill in Preston. When he was twenty-five he won a union scholarship to Ruskin College, Oxford from where he went as a mature student to New College, Oxford. Here he got a first-class degree and has spent most of his subsequent career at the T.U.C. He realises that the union movement will have to change, but emphasises that the changes will have to come from below and not as dictates from above. He also realises that the unions are committed to working with governments of all colours. As he said to Anthony Sampson: 'We created the Labour Party to get what we wanted. Now we've got it, we don't need it in the same way. The Labour Party's job is to get votes. Our job is to get wages.' This is the attitude of the Junta, Ernest Bevin and Walter Citrine.

Index

The numerals in **bold type** refer to the numbers of the illustrations

Acts of Parliament
   Combination Acts (1799, 1800), 15, 16
   Criminal Law Amendment Act (1871), 34
   Parliament Act (1911), 46, 48
   Repeal of Amendment Act (1875), 34
   Repeal of Combination Acts (1824, 1825), 18, 19
   Trade Union Act (1871), 34
               (1913), 46
   Trades Dispute Act (1906), 44
               (1927), 61, 62
               (1964), 89
Anderson, Sir John, 15
Apprenticeship, 6, 13

Baldwin, Stanley, 56, 58, 59, 61
Bank clerks, union of, 87; **74**
Barnes, G. N., 42, 53
Besant, Annie, 36
Beveridge, William, 72–3, 74; **60**
Bevin, Ernest, 55, 56, 61, 62, 63, 71, 74, 92, 93, 94; **44, 59, 62**
Bradford, 1893 meeting at, 42
Brown, George, 83; **70**
Bryant and Mays, 37
Budget, 1909, 48
Burns, John, 37, 38, 41
Butler, R. A., 77

Churchill, Winston, 56, 59; **47**
Coal industry, 8, 56, 58, 59, 61
Common Market, 80; **67**
Conservative Governments, 34, 43, 44, 76ff.
Contracting in, 62
        out, 46
Cook, A. J., 49, 59, **41**
Cousins, Frank, 77; **1**
Craft unions (Model Unions), 28ff.
Cripps, Sir Stafford, 75; **63**

Daily Mail and the General Strike, 59
Department of Economic Affairs, 82
Dictatorships in the 1930s, 70, 71
Dock Strike, 37, 39; **31, 32**
Doherty, John, 19
Domestic system, 8

Economic planning, 80ff.
Electrical Trades Union, 68
Exports, need for, 75

Fabians, 40, 41
Fords, Dagenham, 69; **57**
Friday, Black (1921), 56
     Red (1925), 58
Friendly societies, 16
Full Employment, White Paper on (1944), 73, 75
Funds, protection of, 33, 34

General Council of T.U.C., 83, 88, 94
General Strike,
   Owen's idea of, 20
   (1926), 57ff.; **49**
George, Henry, 41
Gilds, 6, 7
Gold Standard, 56, 57
Gosling, Harry, 54; **44**
Grand National Consolidate Trade Union, 20, 24, 26, 27
Grand National Unions, 19

Hardie, Keir, 41, 42; **36**
Hodge, Frank, 56
   John, 53; **43**
Hume, Joseph, 17, 18, 19; **12**
Hunger strike, 48
Huskisson, William, 18, 19; **14**

Independent Labour Party, 41, 42
Inflation, 78
Ireland, 15, 48

Junta, 30, 33, 94

Keynes, J. M., 66, 67, 73; **55**

Labour Party, 42, 44, 45, 46
   Governments, 56, 74, 75, 76, 82ff.
   Representation Committee, 42
Liberal Governments, 44, 48
Lib-Lab MPs, 41, 44
Living standards, 28, 34, 43, 48, 69, 78, 79
Lloyd George, David, 48, 52, 53, 56

95

DATE DUE			
GAYLORD			PRINTED IN U.S.A.